Nathanael West

Twayne's United States Authors Series

Kenneth Eble, Editor

University of Utah

TUSAS 423

Nathanael West

By Kingsley Widmer

Twayne Publishers • *Boston*

Nathanael West

Kingsley Widmer

Copyright © 1982 by G. K. Hall & Company
All Rights Reserved
Published by Twayne Publishers
A Division of G. K. Hall & Company
70 Lincoln Street
Boston, Massachusetts 02111

Book Production by Marne B. Sultz
Book Design by Barbara Anderson

Printed on permanent/durable acid-free
paper and bound in the United States
of America.

Library of Congress Cataloging in Publication Data

Widmer, Kingsley, 1925-
    Nathanael West.

    (Twayne's United States authors series:
TUSAS 423)
    Bibliography: p. 133.
    Includes index.
    1. West, Nathanael, 1903-1940
—Criticism and interpretation.
I. Title. II. Series.
PS3545.E8334Z94   1982   813'.52   82-11874
ISBN 0-8057-7356-8

For my fellow unmaskers

Contents

About the Author

Kingsley Widmer was raised in Minnesota smalltowns, educated at diverse labors and several state universities, and has held half-a-dozen scholarly fellowships besides academic appointments at ten institutions in the United States and abroad. For many years he taught remedial English at San Diego State College. Among his several hundred publications are seven volumes of literary and cultural criticism: *The Art of Perversity: D. H. Lawrence* (1962); *Henry Miller* (1963); *The Literary Rebel* (1965); *The Ways of Nihilism: Melville's Short Novels* (1970); *The End of Culture: Essays On Sensibility in Contemporary Society* (1975); *Paul Goodman* (1980); and *Edges of Extremity: Some Problems of Literary Modernism* (1980). Semiretired, Professor Widmer lives on the southern California coast and continues to write literary studies, cultural criticism, and poetry.

Preface

When I first read Nathanael West's *Miss Lonelyhearts* as an undergraduate in the mid-1940s, after having slogged through a seemingly endless number of naturalistic American fictions, it was something of an aesthetic revelation in its economic brilliance of style and perception. That provocative novella, of course, also serves as an inverted religious revelation. A generation later, in a chapter on atheistic prophecy in my little book on some issues of Anglo-American literary modernism, *The Edges of Extremity*, I concluded that *Miss Lonelyhearts* was "a highpoint of the modernist American literary imagination." For me, then, West's finest fiction has long been a nuclear literary experience, and that provides my central impetus for writing this essay in summary and interpretation.

This should not suggest that my intermittent rereading, teaching, and writing on West over the better part of four decades have not gone through some permutations. In the late-1950s, for example, I did a survey, "The Hollywood Image: The Southern California Novel" (part of it published in *Coastlines Literary Magazine* [1961]) that rather uncritically emphasized *The Day of the Locust* as the best novel in that subgenre—an argument continued in a cassette-lecture (Everett/Edwards, 1971) and, somewhat modified, in "The Last Masquerade," in *Nathanael West*, edited by David Madden (1973). I now have more reservations, and a partly different critical interpretation, about West's Hollywood novel, returning to the emphasis I made in an earlier essay, "The Sweet and Savage Prophecies ..." (in *The Thirties*, edited by Warren French [1967]), that *Miss Lonelyhearts* provides the most essential sense of West. Surely it is his best fiction.

While I try to suggest several different approaches to West, his fiction, and some of the issues he raises, including (as a critic always should) some negative criticism, I remain convinced of West's importance. Granted, his body of writings, to quote a learned friend, Thomas Staley, "provides a fine and intriguing but still minor canon." It stands as minor, inevitably, because there is only one novella and one novel deserving intense attention. To what degree they may also be viewed as "minor" because presenting an insufficient view of life will be taken up along the way. I focus moderately full chapters on *Miss Lonelyhearts* and *The Day of the Locust.* His first and awkward burlesque, *The Dream Life of Balso Snell,* is discussed in the introductory chapter, following the biographical sketch. *A Cool Million,* West's failed satire between his two important works, receives limited discussion in chronological sequence. I have only incidental comments along the way on West's other work—some weak short stories, some bad screen plays (only several of which I have seen in the form of movies). The long concluding chapter is not chronological but takes up several other ways of considering West and his fiction: reader response, some of the role in America of intellectual pessimism, a partial description of West's humor, and several related issues. But I intend a continuing line of argument, from the introduction and life through the fiction and into each of the concluding considerations: West as the prophet of modern masquerading, role-playing, and its significance.

While, appropriate to this series, much of what I do here comes out as a detailed critical interpretation of the works, my emphasis is broader than the usual summary and explication. History, character, politics, social-cultural thought, all seem to me proper concerns of the critic. For I take the true function of literary criticism to be the annotation of a fundamental attitude, not just the explication of a text but of a significant way of responding to life. Therefore I try to suggest some continuing pertinence of the Westean attitudes, including a serious consideration of his mocking views of much of American culture and society. Not improperly, then, part of my discussion could be considered an apologia for sardonic pessimism.

A reviewer of one of my books disapprovingly noted that I was a "*Weltanschauung* critic"; a reviewer of another snidely announced that I was "a tough-guy of letters." These may deserve quoting (though anonymously because out of context) since the characterizations, though not necessarily the disapproval, seem appropriate. The reader can thus be advised that many consider it not to be quite "professional" to display large and contentious views. Since I have (to use an old street idiom) "taken my lumps" for them, and since academic ambitions are not among my last infirmities, I can with pleasurable disinterest confirm my radically tendentious critical character. Fair warning to the reader.

Since criticism is a properly contentious vocation, it needs no apologies for being so practiced. However, for reasons of convenience here, I have resisted for the most part, directly arguing with the writings on West, though I have read them. A few are responsive, lively, interesting, and, though most postdate my views, I may have learned something from them. As for the rest (say, seven out of ten), they are probably no more irrelevant, pedantic, obtuse, and pernicious than the academic and related writings on most subjects. Perhaps even, to West's credit, one might do worse with a body of reading.

For more positive acknowledgments, I am pleased to thank the generous and responsive Warren French (we have corresponded for twenty years but never met); he suggested both one of my essays on West and this study. Quite unintentionally, two fellowships for other purposes ended up supporting, and providing pleasant circumstances, for part of my work on this study: an NEH Summer Fellowship at SUNY, Stonybrook, for which I thank Professor David Erdman, and a Liberty Fund Senior-Scholar-in-Residence at the Institute for Humane Studies, Menlo Park, California, for which I thank President Leonard Leggio of the Institute. I hope the results are sufficiently learned and sufficiently libertarian to lessen any displeasure they might feel about their fortuitous support. Contra-vanity, I do realize that such opportunities are less matters of merit than of generous tolerance.

More personally, Penny Williams went beyond generous tolerance and affectionately nagged me into doing a better job.

Kingsley Widmer

Cardiff-by-the-Sea, California

Chronology

1903   Nathan Weinstein born 17 October, first child and only son (two sisters) of Anna (Wallenstein) and Max Weinstein, then prosperous New York City building contractor. Family "assimilated" Lithuanian (Russian) Jewish immigrants.

1908–1917   Attends, somewhat irregularly, public schools in New York City—poor student.

1917–1920   Irregularly attends De Witt Clinton High School, New York City, but does not graduate. Summers in an Adirondack camp.

1921   Enters Tufts College on a forged high school transcript. Flunks out first term.

1922–1924   Transfers to Brown University, apparently with someone else's advanced grade record. Bachelor's degree in English.

1924–1926   Intermittently employed in construction for father and sometimes works on his writing. Legally changed name to Nathanael West. October–January in Paris.

1927–1930   Obtains through relatives job as night manager of small New York City hotel. Rewrites earlier material into burlesque novella and starts work that became *Miss Lonelyhearts*.

1930–1932   Relatives obtain for him managership of the Sutton Hotel. *The Dream Life of Balso Snell* published by a small press. Associate editor, with William Carlos Williams, of *Contact*, a "little magazine" where he published stories. Wrote unpublished stories and finished *Miss Lonelyhearts*. In June 1932 father dies.

1933   *Miss Lonelyhearts* issued but publisher soon bankrupt. Lived for a few months in Bucks County, Pennsylvania. Briefly Associate editor of *Americana*, a satirical magazine. Moved to Hollywood as contract script writer for Columbia Pictures.

1934   *A Cool Million*, burlesque satire, written and published.

1935   Unemployed, searching for way to make a living.

1936–1938   Employed for two years as collaborating script writer for Republic Productions on crass movies. Works on Hollywood novel. Writes, with Joseph Schrank, a Broadway anti-war comedy, *Good Hunting* (unpublished), which closes after two performances (November 1938). Active in Screen Writers Guild and "progressive" causes.

1939   *The Day of the Locust*. Well-paid script work for a number of studios. Many hunting trips.

1940   Marries, April 19, popularly celebrated bohemian-divorcee, Eileen McKenney. Summer camping in Oregon. Writes, with Boris Ingster, several highly paid "original" movie scripts as well as other scripting. December 22, returning from a Mexican hunting trip, West drives through a stop sign near El Centro, California, and in ensuing car collision he and his wife are killed.

1957   Collected novels are first published and West's reputation considerably expands.

Chapter One

Masquerading: Introduction, Biographical Sketch, and *The Dream Life of Balso Snell*

Westean Role-Playing

Nathanael West wrote, from his mid-twenties to his mid-thirties, a small body of often intense and insightful prose fiction. The four relatively short books—*The Dream Life of Balso Snell, Miss Lonely-hearts, A Cool Million,* and *The Day of the Locust*—were published during the Great Depression, the 1930s, and often reflect its sour conditions and angers. While his writings received rather limited responses in his lifetime, they became widely recognized as important and influential a generation later. The aesthetic and moral pertinence of his fictions continues and, in spite of the limited quantity and scope of his work, his role in American literary history and modernist sensibility will probably remain intriguing and significant. West stands out.

Some of the most essential insights of West relate to what in his early fiction he called "dreams" and sardonically identified in his last as "masquerades." I view these as an encompassing metaphor for much of what he was doing in his art and life. The masquerading includes what social commentators often refer to as "role-playing."[1] This taking on of fantasy identities involves pretending, for such motives as defensiveness or aggrandizement or inadequacy or belonging or self-hatred or transcendence, to be other than the actual self. Much of it may be distinctly modern, marked by self-consciousness of sexual perplexity and social aliena-tion, an often exacerbated sensibility. One puts on a mask, and cannot completely take it off; the mask takes over. This usually entails acting out dreams and fantasies, often only obscurely recognized as "myths." They can properly be called myths because, as West insists, they are not just individual, private, but historically derived, socially functional, and most emphatically the products of debasing mass-media manipulation and exploitation. The mod-ern mythic process is corrupted, distorted, and fatal. While mod-ern American role-playing aims to be an accommodation to social needs, it ends by denying them. The compulsive charades less create a community than undermine it. Various kinds of violence become pandemic in the unreality. A fantasy identity falsifies and destroys the self it would protect and advance. The masquerades, evident in costuming, politics, megapolitan design, diversion-enter-tainment, and moral-religious beliefs, as well as "personality," become everything, consume all, leaving no adequate reality and no authentic self.

This, as I understand West and his fiction, was a preoccupying concern of his and is crucial in each of his books. Not surprisingly, such role-playing marked his life; he lived in as well as wrote of masquerades. Behind his insistence on characters, and artist, play-ing roles, being the "performer" and "actor" and multiple image and split person, caught up in "dreams" and mass-media fantasies and degenerated mythic *personae*, lay a sometimes anguished and divided but also humorous self-consciousness. Perplexed self-con-sciousness provides much of West's subject and is certainly the source—and some of the effect—of his rigorously hyperbolic style. As a fictionist, West is both a masquerader and a masquerade breaker, wildly fantasizing and sardonically attacking fantasies. He puts forth large "dreams"—of modernist art, Christianity, the American gospel of success, and mass-romanticism—while exposing them as masturbatory, escapist, fraudulent, violently vengeant, catatonic. Such paradoxical involvement with fantasies must draw on guilty intelligence, on his own pretensions to art, morality, success, romanticism. Only an uncertain role-player could be so angry about role-playing, treating it simultaneously with empathy and with savagery—a love-hatred of masquerading which, at its best, achieves a compassionate iconoclasm. It is this distinctive attitude which I want to pursue through much of West.

The Fractured Masquerade of the Life

Nathanael West was born Nathan Weinstein in New York City in 1903. His parents, Max and Anna (Wallerstein), had immigrated to New York, apparently in the 1890s, from Russian Lithuania in one of the great later Jewish exoduses. Max Weinstein, along with other family members, followed the kin-traditional building construction business, and prospered. His only son, Nathan, seems to have been raised in affluent circumstances by a warm family. He apparently was, as they used to say, a "spoiled" kid, indulged and self-indulgent. Perhaps that encouraged the play of fantasy.

But imagination may be better grasped in terms of its obstacles. One of the more important conditions of West's childhood and youth, as I view the social and biographical evidence, was the ambivalence of the "assimilated" Jewish-American.[2] This social-psychological double-bind, widespread among the second generation Jews of eastern European origins, seems to have partly arisen from anxious mainstream American identification undercut by a sense of difference, including some enforced separateness. Anti-Semitism, which had been part of the reason the Weinsteins fled Russia, continued in the United States. However mild by comparative historical standards, it was nonetheless pervasive in early twentieth-century America. West, it seems evident from his fiction as well as from biographical reports, did not escape the fear, the anxiety, and the denigrating self-consciousness which result from such historic prejudice.

Some social paranoia, not surprisingly, becomes deeply ingrained in the sensibility of the victims of bigotry. Those aware, as West later was, of the virulent and genocidal anti-Semitism

of Nazi Germany (or of the murderous anti-Semitism of Stalinist
Russia, whose recognition was longer obscured by ideology, and of
other European countries), can hardly be reckoned generally wrong
in their fears. In literal fact, there were widespread conspiracies
to deprive and kill those identified as Jews. Extreme social pessimism, such as West developed, was all too appropriate. His was
to partake of a very ancient Jewish mode, the apocalyptic. Though
a secularized prophet of doom, West in his Jewish paranoia was
prone to forsee the sundering of history and to pronounce, as he
did in his longer fiction, the violent end of the social order. In *A
Cool Million* and *The Day of the Locust*, America is dramatized
as degenerating into a fascist state and a vengeful mob society.
Yet, indulgent fantast and ambivalent self-mocker that he was,
West also presents his apocalypses as ironic prophecies, horrendous
jokes.

The joking bitter prophet, though hardly confined to the Jewish
(compare the outsider-mockers, from Diogenes on, or gallows
humor), does have an ancient Semitic lineage. Doom, as it were,
had been going on for a long time. A sense of part of one's identity
as involved in ancient persecution and other peculiarity gives an
insecurity both defensive and aggrandizing. This included, especially
among the somewhat cultured (as were the Weinsteins), an
anxious intellectual assertiveness and ambitiousness, a push toward
"universality" which no doubt has deep historic religious origins;
hence, perhaps, some of the identifiable Jewish concern with large
issues and roles. Yet ambivalent self-consciousness about a lineage
and recurrent reality of persecution and outcastness and suffering
may make any prophetic mission bitterly ironic.[3]

The clowning prophet, whether in contemporary Jewish-American fictions (such as Saul Bellow, Phillip Roth) or standup
comedians (such as Lenny Bruce, Mort Sahl), combines an awareness of impending doom with self-consciousness of his own marginality. High seriousness comes out as self-denigration, the prophecy, and the prophet, both exalted and mocked. West may be seen
as both exalted and mocked in his family role as only son and
eldest child of success-oriented and nonpious Jewish immigrants

in America, whose ethos he seems to have somewhat ambiguously
rebelled against. Apparently a bright, dreamy, and gangly child—
six foot when grown (tall for that time) but ill-coordinated—
West, with early receding dark hair and large nose (most of his
adult life he wore a partly disguising large mustache), and physically awkward and slow (his ironic adolescent nickname was
"Pep"), may have thought of himself as Jewish-homely. Not
uncommon one and two generations ago, this was a secondary
manifestation of the saddest vengeance of prejudice—self-hatred
(as Richard Wright and others were also to tell us about being
black in white America). Otherwise put, Nathan, as a bright and
intense child of a doting and ambitious family, thought too well
of himself; as an awkward and homely Jewish boy in a bigoted
gentile society, he thought too ill of himself.

The favored only son, and romantic adolescent, seems to have
found Jewish identity a problem not only in his variance from
stock Anglo-American physical appearance and style but in being
barred from such fatuous acceptance as Ivy League fraternities.
Apparently, too, he was burdened with his mother's expectations
of Jewish identification and commercial success. West's anti-
Jewishness, which would thus seem to have been both aggrandizing and defensive, was emphatically noted by several Jewish
friends. As his cultivation increased, he seems also to have insistently linked Jewishness with the nouveau riche vulgarity he treated
with aesthete disdain. Probably compensatorily, in his later adolescence he elaborately cultivated a monied conservative social
image (Brooks Brothers clothes, etc.), even to the rolled umbrella
and unexpressive demeanor. The descriptions of West in his early
twenties give a dandified and noncompetitive posturing, a reticence
combined with considerable mystification—he was quite a liar—
and note non-Jewish sexual relations and anti-Semetic remarks and
jokes (they also compulsively appear in all his books). While he
always remained devotedly involved with his mother and sisters
and a number of Jewish friends, he seems to have insistently had
non-Jewish girl friends; he later married a gentile; and he avoided
most Jewish religious, cultural, and social affirmations. Or so he

wished to appear, as part of his masqueraded Jewishness. He also took on a number of roles, in and out of his fiction, rather antithetical to his Jewish background. At the age of twenty-two he legally changed his name from Nathan Weinstein to the more Americanly poetical (indeed, quaintly *goyische*) Nathanael West. He is reported to have explained that he took literally the famous American advice "Go West, young man!"

In such psychic geography of alienation—and not a little paranoia about mainstream American society—we can recognize some Jewish role-playing as the ironic intellectual. Yet West played an even more gentile role as a student. While the Weinsteins seem to have had some of the traditional eastern European Jewish admiration of learning, from an early age Nathan was an insistently truant and indifferent student in the public schools of New York City. He would not play the role of the "smart Jewish kid." This continued through De Witt Clinton High School, which he attended from 1917 to 1920 without graduating. While interested in playing ball, as at a boys' camp in the Adirondacks where he spent a number of summers, he seems to have been awkwardly poor at it. Given that time and place, this may have increased the sense of alienation; it may also have encouraged in his anxiously indulgent family circumstances West's sardonic self-mockery, some compensatory exotic artistic-literary interests, and an insistent need for conning the system of the mainline society. He would, after all, in however left-handed a way, play the smart Jewish kid. Those balls he could catch.

Thus not yet eighteen or a high school graduate, West nonetheless got himself into Tufts College, apparently on the basis of a forged high school transcript. Yet refusing to play the student, he flunked out the first term. The following term (1922), he also conned his way into Brown University, apparently on the basis of the advanced grade record from Tufts of someone with a similar name but more conventionally studious habits. Thus disguised on the records as a smart Jewish kid, he could slide through most of his college requirements without playing smart. The double play worked and West managed to graduate, rather barely in what was then thought of (by upper-middle-class gentiles) as a gentlemanly way, two and a half years later with a bachelor's degree in English (1924). One unfortunate price of the collegiate masquerading was that he had rather permanently acquired some of the Ivy League mind set, including mannerisms and tastes of the genteel-rich (costuming, hunting, fancy consumer extravagance) and certain smug snobberies which would appear at times in his fiction. Such is a usual crippling of sensibility by that "assimilating" role-playing.

While at Brown West seems to have been mostly an irregular and poor student, but he did develop out-of-class interests in rather mannered learning, including modernist literature and art, and related role-playing. He appeared as a sometimes striking campus dandy and a roisterer active in several undergraduate literary groups (he published in the college literary magazine). While he could booze and carouse with the gentiles, though not get in their fraternities, his closest associates included clever Jewish aspirants to literary roles, such as S. J. Perelman, who became a lifelong friend. West was to continue such contradictory role-playing of the smart Jewish kid in partial disguise, a costuming which ironically confirmed the original identity. The literary life, with which he had started to identify, seems to have served similar displacements. As with a considerable number of sensitive young Americans of the last several generations, the labyrinthine-romantic roles of the modernist artist may have appealed as a way of escape from the ordinary social roles, as an insider affirmation of an outsider identity, even as a transcendence of self-hatred. There, in the exalted privateering of vanguardist art, were heroics for uncertain alienation, iconoclasm, and personal muddles, a community for otherness in a grossly defining America, and an appearance of profession for those without clear and acceptable purpose.

But in good part West's postcollege roles remained marginal and ill-defined. For several years he lived with his family, working intermittently in construction in New York City for his father, and struggled with burlesque-confessional writings. With family support, he spent about three months in Paris at the end of 1926—

a time and significance he apparently much exaggerated in later accounts of it. Partly that may have been because of his desire to role-play the 1920s aesthete and to substantiate his surrealist stance. More toughmindedly, we might also note that literary vanguardism has also often served a defiant refusal of maturity—a point West was to confessionally insist upon in his first published novella. An aspiring writer, of course, did not have to go to Paris to acquire a dada-surrealist sensibility—West seems to have been reading of and in it in "little magazines" for some time—but the Paris sojourn was then a fashionable, and not terribly expensive, thing for the artistically inclined role-players. Surrealism did influence West's writings and furthered his developing tastes for iconoclasm and the absurd.

But his tangible life remained rather more mundane. Biographers' descriptions of West's family relations suggest the stereotypical Jewish mother—anxious, possessive, success-oriented, nagging, demanding—and two doting younger sisters, with the mild father declining in finances and health (he died in 1932). West partly distanced himself from his family when relatives obtained for him in 1927 a job as night manager of a small Manhattan hotel. His beloved youngest sister, Laura, married his college friend, S. J. Perelman, an increasingly successful comic writer, and West developed a strong dependence on them. (His third novel was dedicated to his brother-in-law, his last to his sister.) West slowly rewrote his burlesque confessional novella, whose origins probably went back to his college days, and *The Dream Life of Balso Snell* was published by a small press in 1931. Though literary response was slight, West, a frequenter of stylish New York bohemian circles in this period, seemed committed to finding a literary role. He had also started to write a much more serious and ambitious work which was to become *Miss Lonelyhearts*.

In 1930, relatives with an interest in the Sutton Hotel in New York obtained for him a job as manager, apparently a comfortable living. The following years were also his most active in serious literature. He became energetic associate editor, under the encouraging William Carlos Williams, of a little literary magazine, *Contact*, which appeared for three issues in 1932 before expiring. There he published some preliminary material for *Miss Lonelyhearts,* as also in another little magazine, *Contempo.* In 1933 West was briefly an associate editor of *Americana,* a satirical magazine. Clearly, he had cultivated many literary "contacts." During this period he also wrote a number of unpublished, apparently rather sketchy and jokey, stories. The much rewritten *Miss Lonelyhearts* was published by a commercial press in 1933. It had some responsive reviews—indeed, might be considered a *success d'estime* for that time—but publishing problems, the Great Depression, and of course the book's artistic seriousness, resulted in very poor sales, though the movie rights were sold to Twentieth Century Pictures. (A bad, dimly related movie, *Advice to the Lovelorn,* was soon made from it; in the 1950s, Dore Schary made the movie *Miss Lonelyhearts,* with Montgomery Clift, which was more related to the novel but also badly done in its heavy pathos and portentous lack of wit.)

The Masquerades of the Later Life

At thirty—a watershed time for many American males—West apparently felt himself committed to his role as a writer. But other aspects of his life seem to reveal considerable uncertainty—abortive love affairs, dissatisfaction with the hotel managing job, and (if I read rightly the comments of those who knew him) responses which were an odd mixture of lively geniality and harsh pessimism. Wishing to escape from the hotel, where he resided as well as worked, and perhaps to play a more class-mysterious countrified role, he bought (with the Perelmans) a farm in Bucks County, Pennsylvania, where he lived and wrote for a few months before permanently leaving the hotel. The Hollywood connection through the sale of *Miss Lonelyhearts* led to a short-term job as a subordinate script reviser (Columbia Pictures). Working on sleazy romantic films, this antisentimental contemner of popular American mythology had found, though he may not have known it then, a regular masquerading role.

While West returned East in a few months to complete and publish his burlesque satire of American success, *A Cool Million* (it sold poorly except for the movie rights), he went back to Hollywood in 1935 where he finally obtained regular employment as a hack writer (for Republic Productions)—his own burlesque success. While making a quite comfortable, even for those times lavish, living by writing crass studio stuff, he solaced himself in his role as a serious writer by working on a satiric study of Hollywood which was to become *The Day of the Locust.*

West also tried for another commercial writing role; with another screen writer (Joseph Schrank) he did a jokey antiwar comedy for Broadway, finally entitled *Good Hunting,* which closed after two performances (November 1938) but was also sold to a movie factory.[4] For the following two years, West was not only an increasingly well-paid script writer for several studios—he never worked on films of any quality or enduring interest—but also collaborated (with Boris Ingster) on free-lancing pseudo-original scripts which were sold for very considerable sums. As with his schooling, there was more than a touch of the con man in West's script writing. He was, in a later idiom, a rip-off artist of more than average success, though he had not made his cool million.

While well-established in the entertainment industry, West seems to have viewed much of it with contempt, reasonably enough. Still, the need for his Hollywood hack role seemed confirmed for him by the mixed reviews and poor sales of *The Day of the Locust* in early 1939. He did vaguely talk of another novel. Whether he would have written it if he had lived longer can only be a speculative issue, since he seems to have done no serious writing in the last two years after completing his Hollywood novel. Apparently he still justified his role as hack writer as support for the serious artist. Or was it, as often happens, and especially in the Hollywood of that time, really the other way around—the pretense at seriousness justifying the engagement in intellectually debased hackery?

There were other distractions than his exploitative script writing. One was marriage in 1940 to Eileen McKenney, a twenty-seven-year-old divorcee with a young child. For the times, she was a bohemian figure of some celebrity (from the popular sketches, later a play, by Ruth McKenney, *My Sister Eileen*).[5] West was nearing thirty-seven at his first marriage, after several ambiguous moves around matrimony in earlier years. The evidence suggests that, in the rather stock Oedipal way of those times, he had a badly divided view of women which included the traditional male-bigot "double standard." In one direction, West shows a fearfully worshipping relation to mother, sister, etc.—the work of the incest taboo (especially strong in Jewish culture), the Freudian would say. And he apparently had the reverse, a fascination-repulsion toward prostitutes, from whom he may have gotten gonnorhea a number of times. Possibly West's late marriage to a sexually experienced woman was what is called "a good one," but all his serious writings were earlier. In them, female sexuality tends to be fascinatingly horrific, women destructive powers demanding hostile responses. In the fiction, there is also a strong motif of ambivalent homoeroticism (the biographers have not explored the subject in the life). Masturbation, rape, and degradation fantasies take a crucial role in the stories, and sexual arousal is usually brigaded with violence. West's sex-violence obsessions in his fiction may suggest erotic difficulties in the life.

We may also recognize a deep psychological dramatization which links the fear of the female with another role West obsessionally pursued—the Nimrod. He was an ardent hunter (and to a lesser degree, a sports fisherman), which was certainly odd for a sensitive and artistic urban Jewish young man of that time. In American he-man culture, sport hunting, among its other curious gratifications (including often a camaraderie of homoerotic dimensions), carries a virility proving or compensation. With West, as with the rather different sporting mythologies of Hemingway or Faulkner (with whom West hunted in California), some misogynistic elements seem evident. West, anyway, was a near-fanatical hunter, shooting all sorts of game up and down the West Coast, and he spent many weekends, vacations, and his honeymoon, so engaged. Reportedly, he slept with his hunting dogs; he lavished attention and money on special guns, duck decoys, and other equipment; and he was a lively—and of course fanciful—hunting anecdotalist. While it is considerably true that American males of past generations did not know how to go out into "nature" without carrying a weapon—one needed a gun as an excuse for taking a walk in the woods, an image carrying back to the frontier— we may also recognize other elements in West's obsession. As will be noted in several of the fictional works, West did not have a sentimental view of the landscape, and there are some qualities of horror-fascination in his responses to nature and action in it. Natural scenes reveal no less a sense of alienation, of harshly indifferent universe, than grim urban chaos. Yet within the aliena- tion, playing the all-American Nimrod, dandifying blood sports, may also have been for West a crucial role of overidentification with the obscurely different gentile culture and its "manliness."

Even more problematic, in my view, were some of West's political responses. Leftist politics played a major role in the later years of his short life. As near as I can tell, in college and the following years West's political responses seem to have been the antipolitics so often yoked with the literary modernism of the 1920s, including an aesthete's revulsion to mass culture and dis- order, a dadaist-surrealist cynicism and *epater* of the cultivated bourgeois, and a strong compassion (however twisted and de- fensive) for suffering. This, of course, is an individualist politics of a kind, however antithetical to more earnest views. Yet, after his first novella, West was also a writer obviously responding to his time and place, the depression and fascist 1930s. While I do not clearly see any watershed point of "social consciousness" (as it was called then), sometime in the early 1930s the aesthete— individualist of the 1920s became a political leftist, and the com- mitment seems to have accelerated over the depression decade, especially under the influence of Hollywood leftism.

West's leftism, as I shall argue later, is more evident and im- portant in his fiction (at least in his two longer works) than many commentators have been willing to acknowledge. Perhaps they partly do not because the politics tends to violate other prem-

ises of the fiction, thus marring the works. While West's politics
seem less emphatic in his writings than in those of many of his
literary friends, and other contemporaries, they may still be a
crucial context. Not surprisingly, many of West's literary friends
throughout the 1930s were well-known "fellow travelers," such as
Lillian Hellman, Jack Conroy, and Michael Gold, though some
(especially in the earlier years) were more independent leftists
such as Edmund Wilson and James T. Farrell. Other friends, including his "in-laws," were also active "progressives." In Hollywood, West was an early member of and active in the Screen
Writers Guild, that curious professional union which most disinterested commentators agree was for long pretty much dominated
by the Communist Party. A biographer reports that he was on the
guild's Executive Board in 1939.[6] Certainly West participated in
"Popular Front" activities: a Stalinist-dominated writer's confer-
ence, at which he spoke; support efforts for the Spanish Republi-
cans; and aid for the exploited white migrant farm workers of
the time in California. West took Marxist "instruction" (indoctrination preparatory often to Communist Party membership), and apparently patched-in stock leftist ideological bits in several film
scripts (see, for example, *Five Who Came Back,* scripted with
Dalton Trumbo and others). While not reported historically as a
major fellow traveler, West certainly seems to have been deeply
involved.

Given an earnest political awareness of the depression and
expansive totalitarianism, his writer friends and many of his
Hollywood associates, and perhaps some of his background and
his other guilt about his hack work and relatively affluent circumstances, this ideological activism was in that time and place
conventionally honorable. It was also not a little hypocritical, as
with many of the other exploitatively successful screenwriters (and
others) in Hollywood turning out gross American entertainment-
indoctrination. I also detect in West's fellow traveling a somewhat
forced role—humor and irony notably absent—and suspect him of
political-moralistic role-playing as well as some other opportunism.

But what strikes one as more deeply ugly in West's political concern for some kinds of social justice was an apparent absence of any revulsion against Stalinism (or its purges, enslavements, assassinations, the Moscow Trials, the Hitler-Stalin pact, etc.). Nor can I find any negative response on West's part in his last years to the American Communist Party's trickery, power plays, and cultural grossness, and all the other betrayals of leftism, including the persecution of other dissidents (for example, Trotskyists), and the pervasive intellectual dishonesty and violations of decency. West, then, in spite of his skeptical aestheticism and sardonic pessimism, was an ardent "progressive" (the word appears in this sense in several of his letters), i.e., a devoted Stalinist fellow traveler. Or at least he thoroughly played that role. Surely some of the moral motives were compassionate (though some could also have been opportunistic), but he may also be seen as a victim-perpetrator of a political masquerade.

West did not live until the major unmasking. He died before the further Stalinist ideological costumings of World War II—the "Allies" in the supposedly virtuous crusade against fascism—and the "Cold War" involutions of Soviet and American imperialism, and the tortuous intellectual fellow traveling on both sides. Hollywood friends and associates of West's went through the House Un-American Activities Committee nasty exposés of film-industry writers, and others, the "blacklisting," the McCarthyite opportunistic persecution of the dissident and not so dissident, and the rest of that grotesque history. In the 1970s there developed some post–Vietnam War disillusioned circling back, a fashionable partial rehabilitation in which leftist-liberal ideology about Stalinists and fellow travelers of the earlier period gave them an almost heroic aura. West's name and role marginally appears in some of these accounts. While not so mean-spirited as earlier phases of the left political fable of illusion-disillusion-reillusion, it may be a proper focus for melancholy reflection. In large part, those Stalinists and fellow travelers of West's generation were deluded people. Those among them who were successful, and highly paid, script writers, union officials, and other professionals, were no doubt considerable hypocrites in their ostensible concerns for social justice. While

there could be a partially positive accounting for their concerns—
the Spanish Republic possibly merited support even after the Stalinist takeover; the plight of the California farm workers was genuine
—and still is; fascism certainly deserved resistance, though World
War II probably as much furthered totalitarianism as resisted it—
there may also be much negative accounting due. These were often
unlibertarian people who tended to support authoritarian responses
(and practiced them in small ways) even when not rationalizing
some of the most vicious politics in modern history. While I doubt
the righteousness of arguing whether covert pro-Stalinism, official
anti-Communism or labyrinthine contemporary anti-anti-Commu-
nism constitute the greater intellectual and moral betrayal, more
authentic liberal and radical responses in the past several generations will likely better be found elsewhere.

West's "progressive" politics, then, need to be treated with
considerable skepticism. But so does much else in his last years,
including his pretty much conventional marriage, his obsessive
hunting, and his exploitative script writing. With all of these, West
may have had little inclination toward serious awareness and art.
Certainly playing Hollywood rip-off hack and duplicitous progressive might not have been conducive to furthering the intense
iconoclastic art of his best fiction. He did, perhaps as part of his
literary role-playing, speak, in some absurdly positive terms, of
writing another novel, though apparently none of it was ever
written. A sense of pathos may be less to the point here than a
sense of irony, though to West those two oddly went together.
Perhaps he should be viewed—commercially, sexually, ideolog-
ically—as a foolish-sympathetic figure out of his own fictional
world, a man caught and dissolved in the many roles he was
playing. After all, one of the most devastating patterns in each of
his books is that no one—not the innocent, not the would-be
saint, not the artist—stays exempt from corrupted and corrupting
American dreams and the self-destroying modern masquerades.
Perhaps he really knew what he was writing about.

West's fiction, with its rather fatalistic pessimism and rather pas-
sive-hysteric point of view, confirms the failure of most roles,

and of the obscured self. West's life, I am suggesting, may be viewed as ordinarily successful—a well-connected and well-paid career of a rather peculiar author who managed to get his odd books published—but also may be viewed as self-defeating in the masqueraded Jewishness and rebelliousness and seriousness. There were, I think, rather forced qualities in the roles West took on as commercial writer and Hollywood con man, as escapist macho sportsman, and as duplicity-serving political progressive. Perhaps one can also find some ambivalence and implicit self-irony in the way he played the roles, all of them a bit suspiciously overdone, as also with his conservative costuming, anti-Semitic wisecracks, and even his literary style. The mocker was self-mocked.

A summary of West's life, then, might avoid the usual senti-mentality, including the pious formulas about literary loss. The thirty-seven-year-old Hollywood hack and sometime novelist, Na-thanael West, and his wife of a few months were returning just before Christmas from a Mexican hunting trip when he drove through a stop sign near El Centro, California. From the ensuing collision with another vehicle, West and his wife died of skull fractures. West's fancy hunting dog survived. So did several small earlier works of sardonically pessimistic fiction about some odd role-playing. It was a fractured life as well as end, a broken masquerade rather confirming the Westean sense of this gratuitous universe and the fragility of the self. And that should be much of the point of our view of Nathanael West.

Unmasking the Literary Life: *The Dream Life of Balso Snell*

Nathanael West's first published book, like the fiction of one of his characters within it, is a burlesque "pamphlet" (less than sixty pages in the *Complete Works*).[7] It may be viewed as an arty masquerade of personal obsessions, both an escape into and a mockery of arty escapism. *Balso* was apparently written, and re-written, over a period of several years in the later 1920s, though its origins may go back to West's college days. In shape uncertain, in tone often archly immature, in form a pastiche of parodies, it suffers from a clotted striving for literary effects and counter-effects. But it has some curious turns and insights. Perhaps most crucially, it mocks role-playing the artist and the fraudulence of literature, religion, and other cultural masquerades.

The Dream Life starts out with a hardly defined persona, a young and vulgar poet with slightly comic-obscene name, Balso Snell, entering the Homeric Trojan Horse by the ass.[8] As we later learn, "The wooden horse was inhabited solely by writers in search of an audience"—as was West. There is a good bit of such self-irony. A heavier sort combines ostentatious literary allusions with scatology: "Oh Anus Mirabilis!" in parady of Dryden's famous royal sycophancy of 1666; B. S. carves pedantic-jokey grafitti along "the lips of the mystic portal"; and there is a fancy mockery of D. H. Lawrence's noted image of regeneration in the self-consuming "Phoenix Excrementi" who "give birth to themselves by evacuating their bowels." Other oh-so-sophisticated allusions, usually facetious and reductive, include George Moore, Charles Doughty, Daudet, Picasso, William James, Bergson, de Sade, Chekhov, Shaw, Joyce, Nietzsche, Rimbaud, Dostoyevsky, Gide, van Gogh, Gaughin, and Huysmans, among others. While some of this seems to be show-offy, two cutting edges also show through: a harsh contempt for cultural pretentiousness and a skittishly pretentious display of modernism. In the rather solipsistic form of *Balso Snell,* the young modernist aspirant slices himself a bit. The satire of the arty role-player—the "performer" he is several times called here—also becomes self-pathos since the attack on the spuriousness of art is done with rather spurious (spoofing) art.

Balso Snell is a literary adolescent parodying other literary adolescents, as with the burlesqued call to the muse, and to the end of Joyce's *Portrait of the Artist as a Young Man*: "O Beer! O Meyerbeer! O Bach! O Offenbach! Stand me now as ever in good stead!" (The final scene also seems to parody a bit the affirmative sexual ending of *Ulysses*.) Some of the parody is more gross. Another literary adolescent, John Gilson, an eighth grader writing exaggerated Dostoyevskean confessions in order to seduce his

English teacher, concludes that he will cap playing "performer" for the arty little theater audience by having "the ceiling of the theatre ... open and cover the occupants with tons of loose excrement. After the deluge, if they so desire, the patrons of my art can gather in the customary charming groups and discuss the play." The trope also plays another way. As the adolescent wrote at the start of his diary, one comes to writing "with a constipation of ideas" for which "white paper acts as a laxative. A diarrhoea of words is the result." Appropriately, then, Balso's first guide in the literary intestine concluded "Art is sublime excrement."

West might be viewed as purging his own excessive artiness with gross rhetoric. But he does not stay for long with the laxatives of ill-digested literature. By a turn of anal sadomasochism he also savages religion with some brief caricatures and mock rhetoric. This runs from some awkward verses of blasphemy about the Virgin Mary and Christ's rusty holes (from the "Jew-driven nails"), through the scatological denigration of a "philosopher-saint Appolonius of Tyana" who keeps a snake in his anus, to "Maloney the Areopagite." That last is a Brooklyn version of the classic Catholic mystic, wearing only a derby hat with thorns and trying to "crucify himself with thumbtacks." He also wants to write the "biography of Saint Puce," a pious flea in Christ's armpit who wrote a rather literal *A Geography of Our Lord* and devoutly died of exposure at the Crucifixion. For West, religion reveals some of the more gruesome forms of cultural role-playing and narcissistic fantasy. By this fragmented exercise in bad taste West also displays some of his lifelong concern with religious morbidity, overlaying his profound atheism.

Equally gross, though hardly profound and certainly digressive, are emphatic bits of Jewish anti-Semitism. The mockery of the arty includes "sensitive young Jews who adore culture," and the scatological denigration of Jewish females, though "Hernia Hornstein" and "Paresis Pearlberg" may at least be better names than the overassimilating "Faith Rabinowitz or Hope Hilowitz." After the guide in the intestinal cavern insists "I'm a Jew! A Jew!" in defensive outrage, Balso replies with some stock clichés of the bigot, concluding "The Semites ... are like the man sitting in cloaca to the eyes whose brows touch heaven" (attributed to the English travel writer Charles Doughty).[9] But West does not pursue such double-take insults, turning instead to relentless variation on other, mostly literary, pretensions.

The motif of art as excrement, by a slight refocus, gets replaced by literature as pseudo-sublimated sex. The adolescent writer John Gilson, partly a parody of Dostoyevsky's underground man, takes on the artist-seer role of writing a *Crime Journal,* but mainly he aims to seduce his Russian-novel reading English teacher, Miss McGeeney. For adolescent art compensatorily serves homeliness and sexual need—"but one purpose, the attraction of the female." Gilson-West also displays self-defeating erotic fear—"I wore my heart and genitals around my neck"—and a larger fear of emotion (the motive force of the parodistic labyrinth): "I always find it necessary to burlesque the mystery of feeling at its source; I must laugh at myself, and if the laugh is 'bitter,' I must laugh at the laugh. The ritual of feeling demands burlesque and, whether the burlesque is successful or not, a laugh...." Reflexive modernist in manner, this rather earnestly pained explanation of the story within the story, part of the inconsistency of tone, more generally applies to West's painfully jokey burlesque. Lacking, say, a Corbière's wit, the self-denigrating laughter often seems forced, a brittle hysteria of the performer within a performer.

Within the shifting tones of the exposure of the adolescent writer also appear several interestingly recurrent ideas of West's. The anality links with a more general compulsion for order, and Gilson plays on one of its paradoxes: "Order is the test of sanity...." Yet in an orderly rejection of his mother, committing a crime, etc., "I order my emotions; I am insane." Hence, in a brilliant understatement of nihilism, "Order is vanity." West will further probe the madness of order in an inherently disordered world in *Miss Lonelyhearts.* Also recurrent there will be the distorted homoeroticism played with here. The imaginary crime the adolescent presents, the stabbing while nude of an idiotic dishwasher whose manners offended him, not only takes off on Dostoevsky's *Crime*

and Punishment but on Gide's antireligious *Lafcadio's Adventures.*
In the gratuitous murder, West dramatizes homosexual excitement
and guilt in an insistent and recurring concern with sexual
ambivalence.

In John Raskolnikov Gilson's other story, "The Pamphlet,"
West plays upon other ambivalences. Gilson's imaginary mistress,
Saniette, dies refusing to face up to that other physical reality,
death. She also drives Gilson to obsessional "extraordinary" behavior to compensate for sexual disgust and neurasthenia. Saniette
blandly accepts his beatings when persuaded they have "high"
literary justifications. The degraded literary-erotic catharsis—"O
constipation of desire! O diarrhoea of love!"—also releases in
forced laughter at an anguished self-division of the yearning but
physically repulsed artist and a crude sexual "chauffeur within me"
("The Desire to Procreate"). The guilty male doubling further
extends the homoerotic and misogynistic ambivalence.

But West jumps away from the theme of exacerbated self-
consciousness in sexual fantasies to pursue the easier satire of
literary scholarship, as with English teacher Mary McGeeney writing a biography of a biographer of a biographer. Her subject,
Samuel Perkins, four times removed from Samuel Johnson, not
only has a big nose but finally displaces all sensations into smell—
a takeoff on symbolist synaesthesia (*pace* Rimbaud)—even sniffing
sounds, shapes, sex, so that smell becomes all of life. Such are the
odiferous infinite regresses of literary scholarship.

The Dream Life circles rather than develops its physical undercutting of various literary pretensions. The single longest fragmented story within the fragmented story turns out to be partly
Balso's sexual dream and partly a dream of a literary fantasy
by Miss McGeeney who, in nightmare metamorphosis, turns into
Balso's old girl friend Mary (a parody of the Christian Mary
earlier in the dream?). This episode has Balso pursuing "girl-
cripples" because "he had ever preferred the imperfect, knowing
well the plainness, the niceness of perfection"—a justification of
West's own taste for the grotesque? or for sexual degradation and
self-denigration? Balso was made "sick with passion" when he

sees outside Carnegie Hall "a beautiful hunchback," Janey Davenport. With an anxious overdoing, West also makes Janey a hydro-
cephalic, scaly and full of sores, and gives her one hundred and
forty-four teeth. Her hump turns out to be a pregnancy in this
dream displacement of sexual fear and revulsion. Still sexually coy,
Janey demands in trade for her favors that Balso kill her impreg-
nator, the poet Beagle Darwin. Two long letters of his justify
abandoning Janey before leaving for Paris. With smugly brutal
selfishness, he imagines her suicide and his literary poseur's responses, if she had come with him. Here is West's most elaborate
series of early "poses," masquerades, playing on the inability to
respond or otherwise act naturally, spontaneously, simply, except in
disgust and violence, a critique of the modern civilizational malaise
which runs through his fictions. In this, West also employs a
mockery of romantic-pathetic literature, and of his own mannered metaphors, in labyrinthine play with what seems to be some
sort of not quite clear guilt. The bathos turns into parodistically
inflating and deflating rhetoric. An example of the last: "death
is like putting on a wet bathing suit." A more serious shiver
develops with Beagle, Snell-West's alter ego, compulsively playing
literary games. Like Dostoyevsky's underground man, he not only
talks "like a man in a book," but: "I think and feel like one.
I have spent my life in books; literature has deeply dyed my brains
its own color. This literary coloring is a protective one" which
makes "it impossible to tell where literature ends and I begin."
Again, West's earnestness amid the farce underscores *The Dream
Life*'s serious theme of a literary attack on literary masquerading of
authentic response.

Describing his imagined role-playing in a Parisian café after
Janey's imagined suicide, "acting" out romantic and classical bombast, concluding with a parody of Euripides, "Beagle Dionysius
Hamlet Darwin" finally goes haywire as a performer (like the later
dying vaudevillean Harry Greener in *The Day of the Locust*).
"After building up his tear-jerker routine for a repeat, he blacked
out and went into his juggling for the curtain. He climaxed the
finale by keeping in the air an Ivory Tower, a Still White Bird,

the Holy Grail, the Nails, the Scourge, the Thorns, and a piece of the True Cross." Religion, we notice, provides the final absurd arty masquerade; the identifying and supporting symbols become the only reality. For West, one of the consequences of role-playing is that it takes over and becomes a compulsive charade.

In abrupt dream-shift, the formerly "mannish" Mary McGeeney, after acknowledging authorship of the Beagle Darwin letters, gives in to her own reality and lies down in the bushes and spreads her legs. But in yet another escape from authentic feeling into more literary posturing, Balso (as with previous adolescents John and Beagle) goes into an imitatively learned performance. With parodistic pomposity, he elaborates three theorems of hedonism to persuasively justify the sexual acquiesence though it requires no persuasion, except of his sexually ambivalent self. In multiple inflated styles, we get what is essentially the psychoanalytic pleasure-principle, the artist's need for sex experience, and the "Time-argument" (*carpé diem*). However, the metaphysical rhetoric gets overcome by "chemistry" and "an eager army of hurrying sensations," which ends in "one heaving shout of triumph" before his body falls back "victorious, relieved." The end of literary struggle must be sexual orgasm.

But since, according to the title and such structure as the novella has, this is all a dream—a rather damp one—the struggle to supersede literary role-playing fantasy has simply culminated in a masturbatory fantasy. West's literary telescope merely enlarges emotional immaturity. The self-abusing circle allows momentary relief but no breakout, no larger sense of reality in the romantic irony. Often doubling back on itself, also, were the parodies of grandiloquence, classical, romantic, modernist or "popular" (parodistic clichés from love stories, book reviews, advice for adolescents, and stock editorials). To be seriously mocked, they require a context which gives them some reality, but they lack one. West also gives away the uncertainty of feeling by quick switches between fancy styles and gross triteness, esoteric allusions and adolescent jokes of another time ("A hand in the Bush is worth two in the pocket"). The overinsisted upon excremental—a man's swallowing is "like a miniature toilet being flushed"—exposes an obsessional concern with the threatening body, as does some of the sexual detail. The exaggerated imagery strains in its part-earnestness; "through the wood of his brain there buzzed the saw of desire"; his anguished mouth opened as if "laying duck's eggs from a chicken's rectum." But there is insufficient development to maintain the heightened manner. The wit is too often polished down to its raw wisecrack, a symptomatic crevice. The nastiness also seems rather overriding, by which I mean less the scatology and intentional bad taste than the fearful treatment of women, always distorted, repeatedly beaten, killed off. The dream, then, in general as well as in particular scenes, is only partly disguised masturbatory fantasy.

But the onanistic perspective—early on, Balso invokes "O Anon! O Onan!"—in its solipsism never allows entry into a larger meditation and world, though supposedly "reality" provides the base for satirizing adolescent psychological masquerading, religious morbidity, and literary pretension. The work may be seen as inherently contradictory. Part of what is contradicted is the authorial self. West has savaged his own literariness and romantic learning, his big nose, his Jewishness, his sexual ambivalence, his longing-hostile problems with women, his modernist identifications (to which the work testifies), Nathan Weinstein's propensity to role-playing, and some rather obvious guilts. The sense of claustrophobia comes not just from the Chinese-box effect of the dream within a dream but from the evident self-disgusted narcissism. While not just biographical fantasy, the lack of a disciplined outer world pushes the tone to more often sneering at than satire of literature, religion, divided consciousness, and the rest. It is half-serious, half self-indulgent, symptomizing, cultural nihilism in jokey masquerade.

While *The Dream Life* mocks obsessional dreams pretending to be literature, it is also literature disguising-exposing obsessional dreaming. As I will have occasion to discuss again with *A Cool Million*, some essential ambivalence can turn intense satire into self-defeating farce. Perhaps more than he was prepared to recog-

nize, Nathanael West really was John Raskolnikov Gilson hoping
to blasphemously seduce mannish English teacher Mary, and Beagle
Dionysius Hamlet Darwin frenziedly trying to juggle away his
crippling love-hate guilt. Put another way, West may be seen
ostensibly satirizing the decadent side of modernism—the essential
narcissistic falsity (now as well as then) of vanguardism which
does not confront outer reality—but his own romantic involvement
brought him full circle.

Surely bits of the style and perspective are suggestive. The
dadaist tone—insulting the audience, antiart, general nihilism—
and the surrealist manner—dream regressions, the grotesque and
extreme, the rhetorical disjunctions—show not only some wit but
a perceptive assault on culture.[10] But West, like his poet, also shows
himself despairingly stuck in the literary intestines. The pseudo-
journey can lead nowhere. The poignant demand for a direct human
reality, especially sexuality, remains an involuted game of mannered intellectual anti-intellectualism. *The Dream Life of Balso
Snell,* then, provides an ornately self-conscious, and somewhat
awkwardly derivative, assault on what D. H. Lawrence called "the
modern disease of self-consciousness."

Most of what West was to do in his fiction, except for the crucially substantial development of an exterior world, appears in
this first book. The caricaturing and grotesquery were to continue,
as were the artful aggravation of hysteria and the somewhat
clumsy effort to "burlesque the mystery of feeling." Along with
this would continue the astutely perceived erotic fears and the
homoerotic ambivalences. West's later style continues the exotic
aesthetic allusions, the surreal dream disjunctions and the blatant
insistence on what is usually thought of as "bad taste"—the "campy"
(West uses the term in almost the contemporary sense). The
guilty ambivalence of tone will also recur, as in his combined
parodying and exalting of suffering—really an unanswerable screech
of protest against the human condition.

West's iconoclastic treatment of what passes for art, culture,
and religion pervades his work, expressing (however sometimes
labyrinthine or passive) a fundamentally rebellious impetus to the

harshly pessimistic undercutting of all pretensions to adequate meanings in life. The masquerader relentlessly sees through others' masquerades, dreams, costumings. In this early fiction, the dream life of B. S. centers on art. The subject reappears in each of the later books but in a larger context, such as modern religiousness, the crass American mythology of success, and the apocalyptic yearnings inherent in our violent culture and society.

But West's fiction was also to remain somewhat solipsistic, sexually and otherwise tormented, artistically mannered, and centered with ironic role-playing—the malaise incurable. In *The Dream Life of Balso Snell,* his cramped but suggestive early work, moments of desire and brilliant perception can only momentarily break the vicious circle of compulsively ambivalent masquerades. I find particularly useful the suggestion of Onan as the muse of literary masquerading, and the Balso Snell insight can be carried far and wide in a culture that farcially exalts "Creative Writing" and other masturbatory fantasy modes, especially the larger part of its popular culture.[11]

Surely the early set of the Westean way was a negative one; his was mostly the art of demolition. All of his fictions are that, though some in rather larger and more disciplined circles of nihilism. And that probably goes beyond the role-playings, leaving the essential modernist intellectual mission. West's weaknesses, as I have been indicating, are many and obvious, but not least even in them he may be a proper prophet for our culture.

Chapter Two

The Religious Masquerade: *Miss Lonelyhearts*

The Double Play of Profoundity and Pathology

Miss Lonelyhearts (1933),[1] West's second novella, is often, and I think rightly, viewed as his finest work. Possibly some of its superiority to his first novella can be related to the more serious pessimism and concern with commonplace suffering of the depression during which it was written. Certainly it attempts far more than the solipsistic dream-onanism of art of *The Dream Life of Balso Snell*. *Miss Lonelyhearts* is a richly aslant religious fable. The entitling figure, a twenty-seven-year-old newspaper reporter, remains otherwise unnamed than by his advice column appelation, probably to emphasize the forced role he plays. Midway in the narrative, Lonelyhearts tries to explain to his conventional fiancée, Betty, his dilemma:

A man is hired to give advice to the readers of a newspaper. The job is a circulation stunt and the whole staff considers it a joke. He welcomes the job, for it might lead to a gossip column, and anyway he's tired of being a leg man. He too considers the job a joke, but after several months of it, the joke begins to escape him. He sees that the majority of the letters are profoundly humble pleas for moral and spiritual advice, that they are inarticulate expressions of genuine suffering. He also discovers that his correspondents take him seriously. For the first time in his life, he is forced to examine the values by which he lives. This examination shows him he is the victim of the joke and not its perpetrator.

26

Betty still does not understand his anguish, and in her naive but not altogether imperceptive way, thinks that he is sick, suffering from "city troubles," an unhealthy life. But at this point the reader may also not quite understand this slightly stiff passage of the reporter's schematic rationalization. A larger and more perplexed personal and cultural "joke" has also been made evident under the guise of this role-playing.

Part of the Lonelyhearts' victimization comes from responding to the "profoundly" pathetic pleas, the self-parodying letters to his advice column of physical and psychological cripples crying for help: "Desperate, Harold S., Catholic-mother, Broken-hearted, Broad-shoulders, Sick-of-it-all, Disillusioned-with-tubercular-husband," and the many other laments, "all of them alike, stamped from the dough of suffering with a heart-shaped cookie knife." But his situation, on an exploitative periodical in a megapolitan wasteland and under an hysterical cynical-mocking feature editor, Willie Shrike (perhaps named after the predatory bird), makes acceptance nearly impossible, even if he had moral clarity and religious solace to offer.

Nor is any real alternative presented by his fiancée, Betty, "the girl in the party dress" who believes in curative chicken soup, therapeutic visits to nature, boy buys girl a soda, an ordinary dishonest job in advertising, and conventionally cute suburban marital bliss and order. She cannot understand the Lonelyhearts dilemma, nor can all the Betty-moralists of the bland world. For, as Lonelyhearts comments, her "answers were based on the power to limit experience arbitrarily. Moreover, his confusion was significant while her order was not." As long as he takes his role at all seriously, he feels the demands of real suffering. And the lack of adequate answers to it.

West seriously presents the Lonelyhearts dilemma of solacing commonplace anguish; he is a self-defined tormented "humanity-lover." But he is also presented as a grotesque joke, a victim of his own, and traditional Christianity's, pathology. In the third of the fifteen brief chapters that make up the fiction, "Miss Lonelyhearts and the lamb," some of the religious mania appropriate to the "born again Christian" (as we now call it) is compactly annotated. Lonelyhearts has returned to his rather monastic room, solely decorated with "an ivory Christ that hung opposite the foot of the bed," nailed directly to the wall with large spikes, and reads from Dostoyevsky's *The Brothers Karamazov* a passage by the saintly Zossima advocating "all embracing love." Reflecting on his sense of "vocation" as son of a New England Baptist minister, he recalls that "something stirred in him when he shouted the name of Christ, something secret and enormously powerful." Now he knows what the "thing" is—"hysteria, a snake whose scales are tiny mirrors in which the dead world takes on a semblance of life. And how dead the world is . . . a world of doorknobs. He wondered if hysteria were really too steep a price to pay for bringing it to life." Though his intelligent self-consciousness seems considerably greater than the usual born-again religious devotee, the next dozen chapters provide the logic, of his dilemmas and his compulsions, for the concluding "Miss Lonelyhearts has a religious experience" where he feverishly reaches the hysteria of "Christ! Christ!" and "his identification with God was complete." He turns his doorknob and goes forth to "perform a miracle" to test his "conversion," to embrace not only a confusedly vengeant cripple but to "succor . . . with love" all the suffering. But the immediate grotesque result is his semiaccidental death and the messing up of several lives since there is no place for the Christ-vision in the real modern world. Such hysteria really is too steep a price for bringing the world to purposive life since it entails madness, death, and further suffering.

Conversion to faith is the snake-induced sin in our dead world. Lonelyhearts's religious experience comes from a self-cultivated hysteria, aided by fasting, fever, psychic paralysis, hallucinations, added to his personal history of an obsessional "Christ-complex" (his phrase), a tormenting sexual ambivalence, and genuine moral anguish. Also in the third chapter, where Lonelyhearts still just plays with his conversion hysteria, he cuts short his chant of "Jesus Christ" when "the snake started to uncoil in his brain," and pushes himself into an amnesiac sleep. There, however, he dreams that he is "a magician who did tricks with doorknobs ... [which] bled, flowered, spoke." His dream then shifts from such Daliesque surrealism to a Buñuelish hyper-realism in which he recapitulates a college prank. He and several student buddies had argued all night about "the existence of God," then drunkenly gone out to barbeque a lamb, though on Lonelyhearts's "condition that they sacrifice it to God" first. Singing an "obscene version of 'Mary had a Little Lamb,'" they take one purchased alive to a field where Lonelyhearts botches the butchering and the injured lamb escapes. Deserted by the others, he has to messily smash the lamb with a stone, ending with a grotesque Beelzebub image of gruesome sacrifice with flowers, blood, and flies. That stone he will later metaphorically translate into the "rock of faith" so that he can sacrificially offer himself to botched suffering.

Underneath, then, the earnest newspaper columnist resides a sick Jesus-freak, as we would now say. Clinically astute West emphasizes other pathological elements in his protagonist, especially his sexual contradictions. Not only has Lonelyhearts identified with his womanish role-name as lovelorn columnist but his relation to women is peculiar. Much of his treatment of fiancée Betty is hostile, from pinching her nipples to meanly ignoring her to making the virginal girl pregnant to savagely putting her down. Clearly, he does not really like her. He also rather passively lets himself be seduced by an impotent cripple's unfeminine wife, Fay Doyle, though a gross character whom he finds repulsive and frightening (her "massive hams ... were like two enormous grindstones"; "she looked like a police captain"; etc.). She sexually exhausts him, and later arouses his total revulsion. In a final scene with her, supposedly acting out one of his Christian love-roles, he ends roughly dropping her to the floor and blindly beating her "again and again" in the face before fleeing.

He had previously focused on her husband, Peter Doyle, as his Christian love-object, solacing him and holding hands. All Lonelyhearts's sexuality seems messily ambivalent. With Mary Shrike, sex-teasing (and apparently frigid) wife of his editor, he hypes himself into compulsive but always failing attempts at seduction.

Several peculiar obscenities appear here, including perhaps an Oedipal twisting, as in paternalistic Willie Shrike's complaining to his reporter of his wife's sexual coldness before sending her off with him. Apparently, also, in sly lubricity, Mary has Lonelyhearts pet her into sexual response, and then runs in to her waiting husband. But even when thinking of Mary, Lonelyhearts "felt colder than before he had started to think of women. It was not his line." His sexual line seems to be disguised and displaced homoeroticism.[2] While his warmly holding hands with the crippled Peter Doyle might be taken as confused Christian compassion, or at least playing at it, an earlier chapter emphasizes something else. In "Miss Lonelyhearts and the clean old man," the protagonist, after leaving the girl friend he was abusing, goes to Delehanty's, a bar frequented by newspaper people (a pre-1933 prohibition "speakeasy"), where he listens to other reporters tell stories of gang rapes of resented female writers. Then, with another drunken reporter, he torments a gay elderly man they forcibly pull out of a public toilet. Lonelyhearts ends up twisting and twisting the screaming "old fag's" arm until someone smashes him in the head. The sexual fascination has turned into guilty rage. Various other detailing also underlines the sexual ambivalence, such as Shrike shrewdly noting, earlier, to Lonelyhearts, "so you don't care for women, eh? J. C. is your only sweetheart, eh?" (With bemused double play, which West frequently uses, the woman, Farkis, who shows up for Shrike's predatory ministrations right after this is described as an exaggeratedly mannish figure.) As one can confirm in the often effete iconography of the Protestant churches of West's time, much about the traditional Jesus might appropriately suggest a covertly homosexual response. That, of course, should not be separated from the general sexual repression of puritanized Christianity, especially strong in that direction in America, or from the admixture with a guiltily sadistic misogyny. Thus West has larger grounds for strongly implying homoeroticism in the love of Jesus, including the longing for sexual mergence for the born-again in the guise of submission to compassionate feeling. When Lonelyhearts is being most Christian, as with Peter Doyle, he is also being most homoerotic. J. C. does become this terribly ambivalent fellow's deathly sweetheart.

Before turning to other aspects of West's analysis of the Lonelyhearts's syndrome, including the compulsion to order, the violent self-laceration, and the hallucinatory longings, I think it crucial to emphasize the double nature of West's treatment, some of which I have been summarizing. Lonelyhearts is clearly presented by West as thoughtfully earnest about the serious moral dilemma of how to answer and solace hardly remediable human suffering. Other details and tropes confirm that we are to see the young man as sincerely searching for a religious answer to human anguish and pervasive modern disorder. But the reader is also carefully, indeed almost gleefully, provided with the details of guilty sexual confusion, long inculcated religious hysteria, and a religiousized suicidal loss of all reality. The protagonist, and the issues, must be seen as *simultaneously* morally profound and clinically pathological. A good many misreadings result from failing to recognize the careful and thorough *doubleness* of West's perceptions and art. We must see Lonelyhearts as *both* sick and saintly. To West's sardonic non-Christian eye, Lonelyhearts, and much of his religion, can only be viewed as inseparably earnest and grotesque, a pious illness. Modern religiousnesss is a sadly serious disease masquerading as an anwer to the impossible.

Otherwise put, Lonelyhearts is a "case" of denied and twisted homoeroticism, a compulsive-obsessional neurosis, even finally an hysteric-schizophrenic psychosis—a not untypical "Christ complex." But he also reveals the moral quester, the sensitively compassionate man seeking to answer the deepest moral cruxes of human disorder and suffering. He is, indeed, as I first quoted him, the victim of a bad joke, but it is finally a cultural and cosmic one. I think it is this doubleness of view, however finally dissolving into the ironies of the sick saint,[3] which not only produces the intensely paradoxical stylization of the work—combining earnest speech, gross wisecracks, surreal dreams, illiterate letters, witty conceits, serious cultural critiques, clinical detailing, and religious visions—but which gives it much of its distinctive brilliance of perception.

If one seeks the most pertinent literary analogue (the stock literary criticism device), *Miss Lonelyhearts* might well be viewed as a Dostoyevskian fiction. But this would not relate to the Russian's Christian apologetics (a bit mocked with the Zossima passage quoted earlier) but his feverish atheism. Thus Lonelyhearts parallels in part the "antihero" of *Notes from Underground*, another nameless figure also simultaneously a clinical case (sadomasochistic, sexually troubled, guiltily anguished) and a profound existential metaphysician of the limits of rationality and the nature of freedom in an absurdist universe. Both novellas end without any possibility of redemption or regeneration, paradoxical explorations of a fated modernist self-consciousness.[4]

Where Dostoyevsky provocatively indicted the disease of Western rationality as unable to order the self and the world, West provocatively indicted Christian religiousness as masquerading the self and the world. Double playing his material into both a clinical case and a moral exemplum, into a poignant tale and a horrendous joke, West went deeper than either iconoclasm or compassion. It is a profound response to a central issue of our culture.

The Order of Suffering

Suffering is real. Part of what this means for the author of *Miss Lonelyhearts* is that much of human pain, misery, and despair cannot readily be resolved, ameliorated, cured, solaced, dissolved by usual human efforts. In the novella's first chapter, "Miss Lonelyhearts, help me, help me," part of the issue gets established through West's mimicry of three semiliterate letters to an advice columnist: one from an eight-time pregnant Catholic mother in constant pain from her kidneys but piously denied an abortion; one from a yearning sixteen-year-old girl thinking of suicide because "born without a nose—she wants love but finds that even her mother "crys terrible" when looking at her, her father thinks "maybe I was being punished for his sins," and boys won't go out with her ("although I am a good dancer and have a nice shape") because "I have a big hole in the middle of my face which scares people even myself"; and one from the concerned adolescent brother of a retarded deaf and dumb thirteen-year-old girl, with brutally punitive parents, who has been sexually molested. Later letters in the story come from the wife of an impotent cripple, the frightened wife of an unemployed abusive psychopath, a cripple with an unfaithful wife ("what I want to no is what is the whole stinking business for"), an impoverished widow who has lost her son, and a paralytic boy who wants to be a violinist. The problems given are predominantly female and sexual, around physical or psychological crippling, in a context of the moralistically punitive. Such miseries cannot be readily ameliorated, often not genuinely assuaged, and traditionally call for a religious answer.

Alternatively, we find the typical modern response of viewing all such miseries as "illness" which reduce to ostensible corrections by expertise of therapy, trivial psuedo-change, institutional device, or obtuse pity. So with the figure of conventional order, Betty. Even when Lonelyhearts behaves outrageously to her, she assures him that he is just "sick." All suffering comes from a temporary condition of illness. He shouts back at her in moral-religious indignation, though since it is self-conscious it, too, becomes a forced role-playing "with gestures that were too appropriate, like that of an old fashioned actor"—the always insistent Westean point about masquerading. Says Lonelyhearts, "What a kind bitch you are. As soon as anyone acts viciously, you say he's sick. . . . No morality, only medicine." This is the modern "liberal" refusal disguised as tolerance, the denial of the moral sensibility and of responding to suffering, the failure to recognize the unredeemable disorder in the moral universe.

The metaphysical pathos of wishing to restore order, which must of course include responding to suffering, also gets presented in a double way by West. His reporter clearly shows a compulsion, in the clinical sense, for order, an obsessional need to ritually compose things, to restrictively confine sensations, to limit reality. For example, in the chapter "Miss Lonelyhearts and the fat thumb," he found himself "developing an almost insane sensitiveness to order. Everything had to form a pattern . . . ," whether personal efforts, objects in hand, or even the view from the window. But such self-conscious mania leads to an insistent rigidity in which things tend to fall, break, clash, go out of control, as, threateningly, all reality does.[5] In the street the "chaos" seems overwhelming once one becomes so sensitive to ordering: "Broken groups of people hurried past. . . . The lamp-posts were badly spaced and the flagging was of different sizes. Nor could he do anything with the harsh clanging sounds of streetcars and the raw shouts of hucksters. No repeated group of words would fit their rhythm and no scale could give them meaning." Like common little compulsions of counting left steps, avoiding sidewalk cracks, pairing or counting-off objects, etc., the patterned responses will not long hold. The man's awareness of the insistent disharmonies of modern urban sensations is true but has become a madness. All one can finally do with the surreal jumble and cacophony of sights and sounds is, like the desperate Lonelyhearts, try "not to see or hear." Intense awareness, which most of us protectively refuse to have most of the time, becomes a paralyzing condition.

Be it the urban street sights and sounds, a media format (such as the front page of a newspaper, or, now, an ad-announcement-fantasy riddled segment of television programming), or our reality-and-dream garbled mental states, painful chaos threatens if we fully recognize and respond. In a later chapter of despair, "Miss Lonelyhearts and the dismal swamp," the reporter, withdrawn into bedridden physical illness after sex with Fay Doyle, slides into a surreal fantasy, the slough of despond of the modern Bunyan:

He found himself in the window of a pawnshop full of fur coats, diamond rings, watches, shotguns, fishing tackle, mandolins. All of these things were the paraphernalia of suffering. A tortured high light twisted on the blade of a gift knife, a battered horn grunted with pain.

He sat in the window thinking. Man has a tropism for order. Keys in one pocket, change in another. Mandolins are tuned G D A E. The physical world has a tropism for disorder, entropy. Man against nature. . . . Keys yearn to mix with change. Mandolins strive to get out

of tune. Every order has within it the germ of destruction. All order
is doomed....

A trumpet, marked to sell for $2.49, gave the call to battle and
Miss Lonelyhearts plunged into the fray. First he formed a phallus
of old watches and rubber boots, then a heart of umbrellas and trout
flies, then a diamond of musical instruments and derby hats, after
these a circle, triangle, square, swastika. But nothing proved definitive
and he began to make a gigantic cross. When the cross became too
large for the pawnshop, he moved it to the shore of the ocean. There
every wave added to his stock faster than he could lengthen its arms.
His labors were enormous. He staggered from the last wave to his
work, loaded down with marine refuse....

His psychological tics of compulsion, brilliantly extended in conceits by West, merge with religious mania, the phallus become
a cross, and all reality "the paraphernalia of suffering" in a grandiloquent attempt to order our trashy world. Sex and religion and junk
become one tidal-wash of chaos. Against our pathetic futility of
order, entropy wins.

While this compulsion to order comes close to madness, yet
the mania also should be seen as heroic, ideal. In an earlier episode, Lonelyhearts recalled an incident from his adolesence with
his younger sister in which "he had gone to the piano and begun
a piece by Mozart.... His sister left her picture book to dance to
his music. She had never danced before. She danced gravely and
carefully, a simple dance, yet formal...." Though drunk in a
speakeasy, Lonelyhearts is also having a vision: "swaying slightly
to the remembered music, he thought of children dancing. Square
replacing oblong and being replaced by circle. Every child, everywhere; in the whole world there was not one child who was not
gravely, sweetly dancing." The attempt in this, as in the previously
quoted passage, to give geometrical shape and a lyrical and sym-
bolical ordering, Mozartean or Christian, aesthetic and religious,
to our messy world serves high poignancy. And gross irony, since
Lonelyhearts gets in an accidental bar brawl in the middle of his
meditations, and the main real shaping is that his "anger swung

in large drunken circles." He ends up gruesomely assaulting someone, beaten, hungover. Formal and sweet order can have little place
in this world.

A psychologically forced ordering provides the substitute. Religion, in a view such as West's, provides some of the most ornate
forms of a compulsion mania, as with hynotically chanting the
holy name (Jesus),[6] imposing on all the flotsam and jetsam of disintegrating reality the symbolic self-castrating form (a phallus
become a cross), and shaping anxiety with a ritualized routine
(the imitation of Christ). By the thirteenth chapter, after ragingly
beating Fay Doyle in sexual revulsion (and perhaps for not responding to his guilty role-playing with the "love-fruit" of Christian rhetoric), Lonelyhearts retires to his bed for a purgative three
days, living on crackers, water, cigarettes, and hysteria. In religious
crisis and personal breakdown, he attempts to heighten the paralytic
Christian humility he took on a few days earlier by identifying
himself as the impervious "rock of faith." No longer responding
with anger, sex, pity, thought, he wills but one thing in mad
purity of heart, his compulsive rockness. Humility, as so often,
has become hardness. In the extended play with the conceit of the
rock, West suggests how self-demands based on compassionate
sensitivity become its antithesis. Part of the technique here is to
sympathetically see most of the compulsions from inside, from
Lonelyhearts's viewpoint (as with most of the narration, with the
early exception of the physical-religious description of him, and
the late exception of Shrike's last party after Lonelyhearts leaves—
both rather pat foreshadowing devices).

In one of Shrike's shrewd but flamboyantly self-parodying metaphors, Lonelyhearts has become a rock-head, a "swollen Mussolini
of the soul." (Fascist dictator-poseur Mussolini had a very large,
completely bald, and imperviously arrogant dome.) Lonelyhearts's
caring self has become untouchable—it was only "his mind that was
touched, the instrument with which he knew the rock"—so all sub-
serves the compassionate mania to escape from compassion's suffering. His "rock of faith" extends the earlier "stone" of Shrike's
advice: when your readers "ask for bread, don't give them crackers

as does the Church, and don't, like the State, tell them to eat cake. Explain that man cannot live by bread alone. . . . Teach them to pray each morning, 'Give us this day our daily stone.' " Lonelyhearts's daily "stone that had formed in his gut" of moral anguish defensively becomes an all-consuming petrification disguised as faith. He can now desperately but blandly play the calm martyr with all his mockers, even masquerade as the charmingly conventional husband-to-be in advertising-and-suburb with Betty. The obsessional image protects him from all mere reality. "He did not feel guilty. He did not feel. The rock was a solidification of his feeling, his conscience, his sense of reality, his self-knowledge. He could have planned anything." With an amazing doubleness of empathy and mockery, West shows how the call to feeling and genuineness gets compulsively transposed into nonfeeling and masquerade.

In sympathetically savaging the Lonelyhearts mania, West also double plays the culminating religious experience. Back in his ascetic bed and desperation in the final chapter, Lonelyhearts's quest-compulsion reaches madness in which he "welcomed the arrival of fever. It promised heat and mentally unmotivated violence. The promise was soon fulfilled; the rock became a furnace." He is disassociating, a very sick man, and a mystic. The compulsion to order becomes hallucinatory. The decorative Christ figure on his wall becomes moving, animate, Lonelyhearts's "life and light," even apparently his pattern of nerves, as well as the "bright bait" for the dead fish things of this world. Then "the room was full of grace," and he becomes, heart and mind, the fresh "rose" of the mystic tradition of beatitude (and of feminine vulnerability to the masculine deity), and thus completes his "identification with God." The beatitude turns, of course, into a regressive oneness which denies all discrimination of reality and must be fatal.

As I read the Westean metaphors, drawn from the ecstatic Christian tradition, they are both earnest in their intensity and ironic in their jumbling (Christ is bait instead of fish; what the quester seeks is more feverish violence than true serenity; God becomes an approving editor). Lonelyhearts's compulsive imposi-

tion on himself of metaphors of divine order complete, he goes
forth to impose them on the world, to embrace the crippled Peter
(Doyle), the impotent phallus he has betrayed with his wife, arriving on the stairs to threaten Lonelyhearts with a gun to play-
the-man in retaliating for the misunderstood beating of Fay Doyle.
That, indeed, will be the "miracle" of love. Doyle, confusedly
caught between the ecstatic Lonelyhearts he does not understand
and the arrival of Betty, accidentally fires the gun, finishing off
Lonelyhearts in the gratuitously grotesque way which is the only
final order in this world. Compulsive manias, such as born-again
religion, can only feverishly disguise the world until violence sun-
ders all, returning the masquerade to the reality of suffering.

The Solace of Fantasy

Along the way of his quest for religious transformation, and the
fatal masquerade of personal and social realities, Lonelyhearts tries
a pastoral recuperation, a few days in the country with Betty, at her
insistence. Returning from that, especially when they "reached the
Bronx slums," he knew that she and nature "had failed to cure
him" of his vision of human suffering and the need to answer it:

Crowds of people moved through the street with a dreamlike violence. As he looked at their broken hands and torn mouths he was
overwhelmed by the desire to help them, and because this desire was
sincere, he was happy despite the feeling of guilt which accompanied
it.

He saw a man who appeared to be on the verge of death stagger
into a movie theater that showed a picture called *Blonde Beauty*. He
saw a ragged woman with an enormous goiter pick a love story magazine out of a garbage can and seem very excited by her find.

Prodded by his conscience, he began to generalize. Men have always
fought their misery with dreams. Although dreams were once powerful,
they have been made peurile by the movies, radio and newspapers.
Among many betrayals, this one is the worst.

This point about the violence implicit in ordinary suffering (the hyperbolic surreal images) is presented seriously. Since Lonely-hearts feels himself "capable of dreaming the Christ dream," once one of the most serious, he has a fervent stake in the solacing process, and, as a yellow journalism advice columnist, a guilty share in its corruption.

Dream-fantasies, whether of art (the preceding *The Dream Life of Balso Snell*) or of the American gospel of success (the following *A Cool Million*), dominate West's concern. *Miss Lonelyhearts* does not confine itself to the central Christian fantasy; it also sur-veys, as part of its imaginative argument, other dream escapes. The main vehicle for this is Lonelyhearts's editor, Shrike, a somewhat diabolical hysteric-cynic, a compulsive machine for making jokes— a not uncommon repressed type—who exacerbates the Christ-com-plex by making Lonelyhearts the butt of ornate parodies, though hardly more grotesque than the commonplace scene just quoted.[7] Shrike, too, insists on the fusion of the great dreams of the culture and the debasing media—the "Suzan Chesters, the Beatrice Fair-faxes and the Miss Lonelyhearts are the priests of twentieth-century America," which we might update with the whole range of nos-trum peddlers of religiosity and psychiatry. Shrieking Shrike is the angry-hurt idealist about it.

And it is Shrike who, at the end of the opening chapter, mock-ingly dictates the start of an alternative column of advice: "*Art Is a Way Out.*" Eight chapters later, in a series of parody dream-escapes, Shrike proposes more personally to Lonelyhearts "Art! Be an artist or a writer. When you are cold, warm yourself before the flaming tints of Titian, when you are hungry, nourish yourself with great spiritual foods by listening to the noble periods of Bach . . . ," and so on through a nonsense purple-passage and Beethoven and Shakespeare as compensation for poverty and crippling. Thus West continues the mockeries of cultural pretension he presented with his *Balso Snell*, but now the psuedo-compen-satory media culture is viewed, as in the earlier quote above, as gross "betrayal." The exploitative debasement so integral to most of modern culture-marketing has, as with the Christ dream, es-sentially destroyed the ideal possibility for both actor and audience.

Thus we generally recognize that however important the fantasies, the religious, the romantics, the aesthetes, etc., do not really lead lives much different than the rest of us. The great cultural ideals come out as mere diversions, entertainments, psychic and moral masturbations. But is this the "*worst*" of all the many "betrayals" of our humanity? As his examples suggest, West further indicts the processed culture, the exploited fantasy, for a denial of actual reality, of authentic being. Religion, art, and other fantasies now become vicious masquerades in the deepest sense, denying recognition and change of the self and the world.

Denatured religion and art falsify all. So do the other fantasy-answers (though oddly West leaves out our processed politics). Shrike, in the same section as on art as a way out of actual miseries, also provides Lonelyhearts sick-a-bed with other burlesqued escape alternatives. The life of "the soil": "You are fed up with the city and its teeming millions. The ways and means of men, as getting and lending and spending . . . are too much with you" and so you go back to the ancient rural ways and "sow and reap and chivy your kine, not kin or kind, between the pregnant rows of corn and taters. Your step becomes the heavy sexual step of a dance-drunk Indian and you tread the seed down into the female earth. . . ." The hyped-up euphoniousness, the aslant allusions (including Wordsworth, Tolstoy, and Hart Crane), and the emphasis on sexual displacement are all heavily self-parodying. So, too, with escape to the South Seas: "You live in a thatch hut with the daughter of the king. . . . Her breasts are golden speckled pears, her belly a melon. . . . In the evening, on the blue lagoon, under the silvery moon, to your love you croon in the soft sylabelew and vocabelew . . . and when a beautiful society girl comes to your hut . . . you send her back to her yacht that hangs on the horizon like a nervous racehorse. . . ." (Allusions here may include several pop songs of the period and a standard romantic movie formula.) Shrike concludes that the South Seas stuff is done with and that "there's little use in imitating Gauguin" anymore—just more arty masquerade. But let us "now examine Hedonism, or take the cash and let the credit go. . . ." Then follows a cataloging of what we might now call "The *Playboy* Philosophy," with superficial doses of sports, stock vices, faddish paraphernalia, and trite culture ("You fornicate under pictures by Matisse and Picasso, and often you spend an evening beside the fireplace with Proust and an apple.") For your last party, "the table is a coffin carved for you by Eric Gill" (an early twentieth-century English craftsman of neo-medievalizing piety), and you finish with a speech: " 'Life,' you say, "is a club . . . where they deal you only one hand and you must sit in. So even if the cards are cold and marked by the hand of fate . . . play up like a gentleman and a sport. Get tanked, grab what's on the buffet, use the girls upstairs, but remember . . . don't squawk." Shrike annotates for Lonelyhearts this parody (it may partly mock Hemingwayesque American he-man-stoicism) with "you haven't the money, nor are you stupid enough to manage it."

Then follows the parody of art as compensation and passing references to the options of suicide and drugs, concluding, "God alone is our escape. The Church is our only hope, the First Church of Christ Dentist, where He is worshipped as Preventer of Decay. . . ." (While Christian Science provides the shape of the rhetoric, many varieties of faith-healing and escapist rhetoric are at issue, here and elsewhere.) Shrike finishes with a parodistic letter to J. C., the "Miss Lonelyhearts of Miss Lonelyhearts," decrying the difficulty of faith and life "in this day and age," and jokily begging for reassurance.

While this mockery of escapist fantasies has its points, the burlesque testifying to mass-culture vulgarization and exploitation, the manner seems a bit thick, too much in the style of collegiate humor, or *Saturday Night Live*, or certain stand-up comedians. It is an hysterically compulsive humor, a mechanical jokiness— as Lonelyhearts elsewhere comments on professional-journalist humor—out of control in pathetic disillusionment. While appropriate to Shrike in his sexual and moral hysteria (and also to part of the known character of Nathanael West), it is too shallow, too pat, to be really witty.

Shrike's "thick glove of words," typical to a stock type of compulsive joker, self-revealingly culminates in his role as Lonelyhearts's alter ego in his charade party, "Every man his own Miss Lonelyhearts." Also a pathetically anxious sore-rubing are Lonelyhearts's other desperate efforts at escapism—drunkenness, predatory sex, psychosomatic illness, violent outbursts. In his messy little effort at revenge against the tormenting Willie Shrike, he takes Mary Shrike to a nightclub, El Gaucho. He recognizes the phony romantic atmosphere as "part of the business of dreams," of the exploited fantasies of those "who wanted to write and live the life of an artist," or other fantasy modes of adventure, prowess, beauty, success, love—just variations on "those who wrote to Miss Lonelyhearts for help." Mary's insistent fantasized tales of her past and her heritage are just another sad effort at "something poetic" in a meanly empty life. With mechanical desperation, she would do anything to be "gay" (in the older sense)—"Everyone wants to be gay—unless they're sick"—in that saddest of all fantasy compulsions, the anxious search for a "good time." For Lonelyhearts, and the perceptive reader, such efforts can only heighten the "feeling of icy fatness."

Part of the persuasiveness, the seriousness, of the figure of Lonelyhearts comes from West giving him his own sharply intelligent sense of our fraudulent mass culture. Though West shortly later went to work in the Hollywood dream factory, his sense of the "betrayal" by sleazy romanticizing remained constant—the genuine evil which encourages masquerading.

To pursue romanticizing in a slightly different sense, West, in the chapter following Shrike's burlesque of the escape fantasies, "Miss Lonelyhearts in the country," has his protagonist try Betty's therapy of a few spring days with her at an unused farm, her childhood home in Connecticut. This pastoral interlude, which is also the only bit of affectionate sex in West, is more positive than any other scene. Even so, Lonelyhearts finds in a walk in the spring woods destructive entropy at work: "in the deep shade there was nothing but death—rotten leaves, gray and white fungi, and over everything a funereal hush." And even at Lonelyhearts's most vital moment, his copulating in the grass with virginal "little girl" Betty (thus seeing her, he escapes feminine power), he also notes that the small green leaves hung in the hot still day "like an army of little metal shields," and he heard a singing thrush sound like "a flute choked with saliva." While this may partly be understood as West's further characterization of Lonelyhearts's megapolitan morbidity even when in a pastoral love scene, I think it also typically reveals the Westean sensibility. No nature-romantic, he insistently, even incongruously, displays modernist sensibility in its concern with entropic mechanisms.

The pastoral-sexual peace, of course, can only be a regenerative interlude—that is the nature of pastoral—and one hardly answering the "Bronx slums," the letters witnessing horrible commonplace anguish, the betrayed culture, and the megapolitan malaise. A series of ironically surreal scenes in a "little park" in New York City reenforces the point with "waste land" imagery. The park was a self-parody of one, desolate, its ground "not the kind in which life generates," its "gray sky looked as if it had been rubbed with a soiled eraser. It held no angels, flaming crosses, olive-bearing doves, wheels within wheels. Only a newspaper struggled in the air like a kite with a broken spine." For Lonelyhearts, it is a dead land (properly marked by spineless media) but full of inhuman crucifying threats. As he walks through the park, even the shadow of a lamp post "pierced him like a spear." In another nightmarish extension of his anguished psyche in the park, looking toward a memorial obelisk he saw its "rigid shadow . . . lengthening in rapid jerks"; looking at the monument itself, it "seemed red and swollen in the dying sun, as though it were about to spout a load of granite seed." Waiting another sexual rendezvous near the obelisk, "he examined the sky," with the continuation of the same metaphor he had been applying to a woman (a recurrent psychological point in West) "and saw that it was canvas covered and ill-stretched." Trying to fathom its unnaturalness, he "examined it like a detective who is searching for a clue to his own exhaustion." In the "tons of forced rock and tortured steel" that makes up the menacingly surrounding skyscrapers, he discovered his "clue." "Americans have dissipated their radical energy in an orgy of stone breaking . . . hysterically, desperately, almost as if they knew the stones would some day break them." Lonelyhearts's tortured psyche reflects the hard hysterical reality, its revulsive stone becoming the rock that will break him. The park, like the dreams, provides no real solace, only frightening human constructs, stone city and stoned soul.[8]

The mechanically hard and violent order overwhelms all. The solacing fantasies of religion provide no exception. The obsessive Shrike produces a news clipping in a bar—"ADDING MACHINE USED IN RITUAL OF WESTERN SECT.... *Figures Will be Used for Prayers for Condemned Slayer of Aged Recluse....*" Dreams of hope have turned into mechanical bad jokes, media hypes like the Lonelyhearts column, willed and destructive hysteria like the Lonelyhearts "religious experience." They are also grotesquely irrelevant to most of actuality which West, with the pessimistic refusal of solace central to modernist sensibility, sees as harsh, random, breaking.

Violent Tropes

One of the most striking characteristics of *Miss Lonelyhearts*, it should be evident, is the drastic metaphor, the shocking figure of speech. To note a few more. When Lonelyhearts's smug colleague Goldsmith smiled, he was "bunching his fat cheeks like twin rolls of smooth pink toilet paper." When the crippled Doyle hobbled across the barroom, "he made many waste motions, like that of a partially destroyed insect." When hostile-joker Shrike, whose "dead pan" face has been geometrically as well as punningly described, finishes his preliminary seduction speech (religious parody, of course) to a Miss Farkis, he "buried his triangular face like the blade of a hatchet in her neck." Later, when the hysterically joking Shrike tries to persuade the near-catatonic Lonelyhearts, now rocklike in faith, to play one of his mocking games, he "was a gull trying to lay an egg in the smooth flank of a rock, a screaming, clumsy gull." When Lonelyhearts despairingly looks out the window after failing to polish off his column (partly because his religious rhetoric is too drippingly artificial to even be convincing to himself), a "slow spring rain was changing the dusty tar roofs below him to shiny patent leather ... slippery ... he could find no support for either his eyes or his feelings." Often surrealistically hyper-lucid and extreme, the tropes resonate with the themes of mechanical artifice, hysterical masquerade, and violent breakdown.

A number of West's metaphors are extended, in the sense of seventeenth-century poetic conceits. Bemusedly, we hear gross Fay Doyle undressing in the dark for sex: "She made sea sounds; something flapped like a sail; there was the creak of ropes; then he heard the wave-against-a-wharf smack of rubber on flesh. Her call for him to hurry was like a sea-moan, and when he lay beside her, she heaved, tidal, moon driven." And then, as they say of comic routines, the topper: "Some fifteen minutes later, he crawled out of bed like an exhausted swimmer leaving the surf. . . ." (Some critics, again missing the mockery and West's double play, have earnestly misread the metaphoric point as sexual vitality or the maternal sea, but most of West's maritime figures are negative, here and elsewhere, ironic play with the inhuman and gratuitous.)

Some figures more slyly continue. When Lonelyhearts fails to communicate with the embittered Doyles though he has hysterically poured out his Christian-love message (ironically, a parody of Shrike's parodies), he "felt like an empty bottle, shiny and sterile." Half a dozen paragraphs later, his message totally misunderstood by the lascivious and voracious Fay, she attempts to sexually arouse him and he "felt like an empty bottle that is being slowly filled with warm, dirty water." He finally overflows with violent rage.

The elaboration of metaphors, whether of the psyche-stone-skyscraper-city-religious-rock, of the compulsive metaphysic of geometrical and symbolic shapes, of Lonelyhearts phallic fears, breast fixations and homoerotic confusions, or of the parodistic images of media romanticism and debased religiosity, heightens, incises, almost takes over the fiction. Highly artful work, we can certainly believe the reports that West rewrote and rewrote *Miss Lonelyhearts* with a rather un-American sense of craft quite antithetical to the vulgar romanticism of pouring out warmly dirty "self-expression." Curiously, he countered "confessional" subject matter—the dream life of the artist, religious conversion, fantasy-dominated people—with rigorous craft. Almost uniquely in his time and place, West combined self-conscious strict artistry with intense immediate concern.

Some of that self-consciousness deserves further emphasis. West's writing shows an exacerbated visual imagination, beyond his evident fascination with painting, especially surrealism. The hyper-lucid visualization organizes, disciplines, objectifies the concern with extreme subjectivity. Aesthetically, no doubt, West is heir to the symbolists' "correspondences" (Baudelaire), the modernist Anglo-American poets' "objective correlative" (Eliot), and the surrealists' disjunctive images of "dream lucidity" (Breton). But those are pedantic considerations. More interestingly, the self-conscious tropes do something else; they carry out and reenforce the dominant issue of self-consciousness, which is what forces the masquerading. I have noted a few instances in which Lonelyhearts, for all his sincere anguish, is so aware of what he is doing that he has taken on a pose, actor's gestures, a willed role. Even his final desperate escape from consciousness and role-playing by hysteria and hallucination seems incomplete, yet more wilful masquerading. Still another example: in one of his most sincere conversations with fiancée Betty, Lonelyhearts plays what he acknowledges to be a "trick" in speech; "he stumbled purposely, so that she would take his confusion for honest feeling." Ironically, she is too simple and sincere to be taken in. Of course part of Lonelyhearts's difficulty in role-playing here (and with Mary Shrike and Fay Doyle) comes, as I noted earlier, from hostility to women and ambiguous homoeroticism. But it clearly goes beyond that. His self-induced hysterical conversion experience attempts to break through his tormenting self-consciousness in costuming as Miss Lonelyhearts. If he can only become the true believer, the ultimate Miss Lonelyhearts, J. C., he can become real and one, transcend the masquerade.

This I take to be West's crux. Whether Lonelyhearts holds

Doyle's hand as expression of compassion, pursues sex, advises the lovelorn, plans the future with Betty, or withdraws to his rock of faith, he is, as an examination of each scene will show, role-playing, masquerading. The ills of such divided consciousness, and the consequent forced pretending of a role, apply, of course, to Lonelyhearts's alter ego, Shrike, and his ornate joking, gaming, parodies. The "acting" also applies to others, even the inchoate simple cripple Doyle (his pretense at a leering manner in the speakeasy, his playing "dog" for his wife, his later playing the injured husband). Lonelyhearts also applies the point to the dis-illusioned tough-guy pretenses of the other reporters in the speak-easy. They return the perception by seeing Lonelyhearts's religious-ness as put on, made up, "too damn literary." In both details and style West ironically confirms their point. One of Lonelyhearts's colleagues notes that even if the character were to achieve "a genuine religious experience, it would be personal," only, and thus end up "meaningless," incomprehensible, which in fact it does. Another replies that the trouble with Lonelyhearts, "the trouble with all of us, is that we have no outer life, only an inner one, and that by necessity." Then the reporters turn back to compul-sively defensive jokes as usual disguises for their irrelevant feel-ings. But that division between inner and outer life, between hu-man feeling and the compulsive order surrounding it, remains central throughout the novella as the condition of anguished self-consciousness and consequent role-playing—theirs, Shrike's, Lone-lyhearts's, and not least the oh-so-self-consciously artful author's. Our world violates us and we escape into unreality.

Miss Lonelyhearts is also full of small and large violence; stylis-tically as well as dramatically.[9] Violence marks the essential break-ing out of self-consciousness and through the masquerade, a desper-ate assertion against alienation, helplessness, inauthenticity. In his final effort toward religious experience, as I previously noted, Lonelyhearts explicitly wants "unmotivated violence" to restore life to the dead world. And he gets it. Earlier, despairingly drinking and thinking of sex, he summarizes: "Only friction could make

him warm or violence make him mobile." And in yet another
passage, he notes of himself: "With the return of self-consciousness, he knew that only violence could make him supple."

Alive, "mobile," "supple"—these are, in the biblical phrase, the
difference between "the quick and the dead." West, preoccupied
with violence in all his works, which he presents as quintessentially
American, serves it as the assertion of life against suffering: as
when Lonelyhearts recalls accidentally stepping on a frog, and
then frenziedly eliminating its misery by crushing it, or when he
smashed with a stone the misbutchered lamb, or when he twists
and twists the arm of "the clean old man," or when his suffering
over his failure of charity with the Doyles turns to his ragingly
beating Fay, or when his guilty misery over Betty turns to giving
her pain ("like a kitten whose soft helplessness makes one ache
to hurt it"), or when his compassion for the hurt in the lovelorn
letters turns to rage, or when his own total misery leads to the
violent denial of himself. This violently hallucinatory denial of all
reality is the destructive religious fallacy. Violence becomes the
crucial assertion through suffering of life, only to end as its final
masquerade, death.

Among the masquerades which West pursues, one of the most
violating tropes, of course, is the entitling one—the hysterical need
for the ultimate Miss Lonelyhearts. That savage metaphor for
Christianity is truly violent to the heritage, a really "sick" joke.
I suppose that in a vestigially Christian culture it should be offen-
sive to many—if they do not willfully misread or disguise their
responses—perhaps even more so than the fervent blasphemy in
D. H. Lawrence's *The Man Who Died* (a novella written not long
before *Miss Lonelyhearts*) where a Christ copulates on an altar
with a priestess. Perhaps West's more cynical fiction also offends
more supposedly tolerant folk, those from the likes of William
James (*Varieties of Religious Experience* was one of West's
acknowledged sources) to current agnostics. These would grant
that religious fervors have a decently pragmatic side; it is nice
to believe: it may help one feel good, or bear the world, or endure
suffering, or "get through the night," or add other poetic flavor to

existence. Nonsense. For from the Westean view, they may discover that the joke is on them. Betraying self-consciousness and inauthentic role-playing will result in a cosmic pratfall.

While West may be no more sardonically atheistic in his savaging of religious grotesquery than some of his fine artistic contemporaries (for example, Céline or Buñuel), he leaves no room for displaced piety. The role-playing religious order madly violates the (dis)ordering that is. Religion, by the same logic with which it provides acceptance or solace, anesthetizes the essential human and defeats the actual. Instead of answering misery, despair, unmerited suffering, suicide, religion often creates them. To be "born again," as was Miss Lonelyhearts, is to be dead—and quite literally—to the truth. It destroys him, hurts others, answers nothing. Faith is a grotesque disease, however much we are aware, as West was, of the poignant imperatives to it. To falsely order suffering takes the heart out of the human, which would better remain lonely in its unacceptable universe. That is the unmasqueraded message of *Miss Lonelyhearts.*

Miss Lonelyhearts is an exceptionally intense very short novel, yet in the fundamental sense Nathanael West's largest work. Appropriately to its time of depression disillusion (perhaps *the* twentieth-century revelation, so far, that the American system doesn't work), and to its place as a somewhat marginal American's response to the mainline mythologies (Menckenism cum brilliance?), it is a compassionately savage piece of iconoclasm. At the level of stock cultural history, I suppose it can be viewed as combining the zesty art of negation that partly characterized the 1920s with some of the more grimly sordid realities of the following time. As with many of the more interesting achievements in literary history, it does not quite categorize and can be viewed in later perspective as a document of cultural "transition." It seems to precariously fuse two kinds of sensibility—a "hinge" work—with both the artful modern expressiveness of the period after the Great War and the depressed social actualities of the following period— a literary flying fish.

But more importantly, *Miss Lonelyhearts* may be *sui generis,* a striking literary act intriguing in its very exceptionalness for both the times and the author. West's novella may be one of those unique works (one thinks of others by Laclos, Corbière, Lermontov, Zamiatin, Melville, and Hart Crane) which stands beyond its genesis, beyond its author—a one-time only achievement, the small odd masterpiece. Indeed, to continue a discussion of West beyond *Miss Lonelyhearts* must have more than a little of the tone of anticlimax. West was never again to achieve such shaping intensity. *Miss Lonelyhearts* might thus be said to overreach its author as well as times, arriving at that kind of impersonality which certain self-contained works seem to acquire. The "Miss Lonelyhearts" paradigm, as it were, remains a permanent expressive accounting of the religious masquerade, and its relentless unmasking.

Chapter Three

Unmasquerading the American Myth: *A Cool Million*

West's Depression

Nathanael West's third published novel, *A Cool Million*,[1] sub-titled "The Dismantling of Lemuel Pitkin" (1934), puzzles because of its weakness. It shows little of the stylistic pyrotechnics of *The Dream Life of Balso Snell*, though also crude in taste, and even less of the paradoxical brilliance of *Miss Lonelyhearts*, though also violently pessimistic. That *A Cool Million* was, relative to West's other works, hurriedly written in 1933–34 provides insufficient explanation for the book's emphatic disparities with his others since it also reveals little of West's psychological and moral insight, or much other particularized intelligence. It has sometimes been suggested that West may have been trying to "cash in" as a novelist by writing something simple for the popular market. But West's harsh pessimism and political denunciations were patently not the stuff of which successful fictions for the times were made. Not surprisingly, *A Cool Million* commercially flopped. But that the fiction is also an artistic failure—crude in tone, mechanical in form, and mostly trite in both conception and execution of its caricature figures—surely seems inappropriate for the author of *Miss Lonelyhearts*. What happened?

It might be prudent to recall that it is often no easier for criticism to explain, rather than just describe, real failure than to explain, as the old truism has it, "a work of genius." However, I have several suggestions for the failure. The obvious one is West's indiscriminate anger, though playing at a comic stance, sheer rage at America and its failing myths. Failure is also the main subject of *A Cool Million*: the harsh failure of American dreams of opportunity, of poor boy makes good, of the pioneer and Horatio Alger and "free enterprise" moral templates of American success, and of any faith in the saving graces of innocence and virtue. The book is very American in its outrage at this. The moral patterns appear crude and flat, obviously by someone with little sympathy for them. Thus American romantic idealism is not granted the contradictory qualities we can discover, for example, in Fitzgerald's *The Great Gatsby*—or in a considerable number of American lives. West shows no interest in such character, confining himself to contemptuously savaging the romantic ideology in its most naive manner of the American gospel of success.

There would seem to be a bitterness in such scornful telling which demands an external explanation, that is, attention to the biographical and historical circumstances at the time of writing. Indeed, quite a bit of the historical conditions do enter the story, usually in the form of heavy sarcasms. Thus, when the young hero gets a dubious job (as stupidly innocent front man for a jewelry store scam), the narrator adds that after all a job is a job "and in the year of our lord nineteen thirty four that was indeed something." And so it was.

For another example: a Chinese entrepeneur of whorehouses gives up his previous internationalism in services because he "saw that the trend was in the direction of home industry and talent, and when the Hearst papers began their 'Buy American' campaign he decided to get rid of all the foreigners in his employ and turn his establishment into an hundred per centum American Place." Given the Great Depression, that was no problem: "Although in 1928 it would have been exceedingly difficult for him to have obtained the necessary girls, by 1934 things were different. Many respectable families of native stock had been reduced to extreme poverty and had thrown their female children on the open market." The crude exaggeration here must point to a generalized bitterness about the depression which has taken over more incisive perception and response.

Granted, it is an understandable response. For those who do not remember the Great Depression, either because they were too young or because of a fortunate amnesia of circumstances, the socioeconomic collapse of the 1930s may merit a few words of reminder. When President Franklin D. Roosevelt declared in a famous speech that "one-third of the nation is ill-fed, ill-housed and ill-clothed," he was undoubtedly trading on political optimism. A majority of Americans were suffering under a sense of economic deprivation and social anxiety. Even those who were not felt burdened with a great fear of worse coming, even unto political collapse, as apparently did the author of *A Cool Million*. This is not just a matter of how many were hungry—there were quite a few—or what proportion were unemployed or miserably employed—it has never been higher in American history—but of a more general sense of malaise. The "system" did not seem to be working. From right and left, it seemed to be terribly unjust. The palliatives, over a number of years, did not really work, meet the basic needs. Indeed, the American economic system never did work the same way again. The depression only ended with the full-scale militarism of World War II, and with the welfare-warfare statism that has been a dominant characteristic of the American socioeconomic order and faith since then.

Much of the old American way had ended—a point that *A Cool Million*, with an almost too obvious moral indignation (after all, it was overdue) beats upon. It is generally agreed by commentators on the 1930s that the depression was psychological and ideological as well as economic. It included the breakdown of many popular American ideals, and illusions. This is much of what West focuses on in *A Cool Million*, only thinly disguised (contrary, I think, to many portentous commentators) as a mockery of American myths of innocence. Such disillusion was the bitter subject of much of the more significant writing of the depression years, especially the year of West's novel, 1934. And this appears whether the material was the poetic reportage of expatriate down-

and-under life, as in Henry Miller's *The Tropic of Cancer*, or the political-uplift allegories of the "proletarian" novel, as in West's friend Jack Conroy's *The Disinherited*. (It did not, of course, end in 1934, as with the later sentimental-naturalism of John Steinbeck about the poor [1938], or, say, the poetic-documentation of impoverishment of James Agee's *Let Us Now Praise Famous Men* [1941].) Most such works reveal not only that the socioeconomic order had gone to pot but a larger rage of disillusionment. Many of the self-conscious reacted bitterly, sometimes in obvious inversion of the orthodoxies of American culture, the Couéism, boosterism, and other shoddy pieties of the 1920s optimism. The Great War and Great Depression were collapsing ideas of "Progress" and positiveness, as were the spreading European ideologies of demystification—Freudianism, Spenglerism, Marxism (all evident influences on West). Modernism in the arts, with which West fervently identified, had long been insistently antibourgeois, myth shattering and iconoclastic, pessimistic.

Furthermore, the Weinstein family's prosperity had considerably declined in the later 1920s. West's work in small New York City hotels confronted him with defeated, and sometimes suicidal, cases of the despair of the times. West's own circumstances as a writer were not promising. His once-successful and hopeful immigrant father had died. And not least, I suspect, the erotically perplexed West had reached that male watershed age of thirty. Combining these with the moral climate of the time, and a new political emphasis (to be discussed later), it is not surprising that West would write a bitterly angry exposé of depression America.[2]

All-American Parody

The narrative pattern of *A Cool Million* takes off on the previously popular stories of virtuous poor boy makes good, exemplified by the trashy best-selling fiction of a generation earlier of Horatio Alger, though of course such simple-minded success fantasies were widespread in America. Lemuel Pitkin, seventeen-year-old son of a poor aging farm widow, Sarah, living on the Rat

River near Ottsville, Vermont, is endlessly innocent and virtuous, in a moronic way (no double view of the protagonist here, as in *Miss Lonelyhearts*). "Squire Bird" is about to foreclose the mortgage on the Pitkin place. Lemuel seeks and accepts advice from Nathan "Shagpoke" Whipple, ex-president of the United States (in parody of Calvin Coolidge) and local banker-crook.[3] He pronounces that "this is the land of opportunity and the world is an oyster," so the youth should go forth and seek his fortune. Along with the trashy non sequiturs, Shagpoke provides a thirty-dollar mortgage, minus interest in advance, on the hundred-dollar family cow (on which he later forecloses), for Lem's capital to take to the sick oyster of New York. Most of the narration consists of such facetiously slapdash cartooning.

Before Lem leaves, he is tricked and beaten unconscious by "Tom Baxter, the local bully" butcher boy, who then ravishes Lem's fainted love, Betty Prail. We quickly learn that she had previously, age twelve, been raped by Baxter's father, a drunken volunteer fireman, the night her parents died in their burning home. The orphan girl eventually became servant-ward of "Lawyer Slemp," who for years had been beating her "twice a week on her bare behind with his bare hand." Betty's further adventures include abduction by "white slavers," another rape, sale to an ornate brothel, escape to being a cheap streetwalker in New York, then service as a servant ending in another rape, and finally a not so virtuous end as secretary to Shagpoke who has become a fascist demagogue. This caricature-pornography is mostly presented deadpan, though with moments of archness: "It is with reluctance that I leave Miss Prail in the lecherous embrace of Tom Baxter to begin a new chapter, but I cannot with propriety continue my narrative beyond the point at which the bully undressed that unfortunate lady." In jokey double play, the narrator's trite pomposities often underline the melodramatic actions.

Lem, on the train to the city to make his fortune, is conned and has his pocket picked of his remaining $28.60. But, in parody of the Horatio Alger device of accidental good fortune for the innocent, the con man drops a ring worth a thousand dollars, which

Lem pawns to another con man for $28.60. He then gets arrested as a thief and beaten by the police. He quickly "received only fifteen years in the penitentiary." "It would be hard to say from this that justice is not swift, although, knowing the truth, we must add that it is not always sure." For reasons ostensibly rehabilitative, the warden (liberally applying the Betty doctrine of *Miss Lonely-hearts* that all issues are sickness/health), cures Lem by removing all his teeth and prescribing a "series of cold showers ... an excellent cure for morbidity." (They were, of course, prescribed in Boy Scout manuals and other advice for youth as part of the cure for the "self-abuse" of masturbation, a "problem" then widely thought to be only male; in all of his novels West seems to rather insistently slip in notions and images about masturbation—Balso's dreams, Lonelyhearts's bed-ridden guilts, Homer's compulsive hand-movements, Tod's rape-fantasies).

Further dismantling of Lemuel Pitkin, after his fortuitous release from prison with false teeth and bad health, includes the loss of an eye, a thumb, his leg, his scalp, and some months later, his life. But he never loses his simple faith in virtue and opportunity, or his stupidity. Some of these actions develop from parody of Alger folderol, as when Lem drags a runaway team of horses to a halt just before they crash into a bank president and his daughter. But instead of the traditional boost-up in the world, Lem gets misunderstood and cursed as a "careless groom." He is also tricked by the banker's insurance agent and loses an injured eye. But some of the fictional problem here is not just that West lays it on with slapstick heaviness but attempts to parody an already self-parodied form, the fatuously inspirational boys' story.

West does patch into his Alger burlesque some recurrent concerns of his own of a rather alien cast, such as American violence and homoeroticism. Lem, imprisoned by the Oriental owner of a brothel where Betty is kept—Wu Fong of course "smiled inscrutably"—is forced into a "tight-fitting sailor suit," threatened by a B-movie style closeted guard ("see this gat? Well, if you don't behave I'll drill you clean"), and turned over to a lisping little Maharajah. Almost "swooning" in terror at the sexual advances of the "little dark man," Lem drops his false teeth and glass eye. Such repulsiveness saves him from sex but earns him a beating from whorehouse thugs, then from a policeman he complains to, and then thirty days in the workhouse for disorderly conduct. Sex in West, of whatever kind, usually links with violence and punishment.

Even more generally for West, violence *is* the American order, including its mythos. That would seem to be most of the point of the redundantly presented episode of "the man from Pike County Missouri," a crude burlesque of the "ring-tail squealer and rip-tail roarer" frontier archetype. This hyperbolic "boaster"—described more genially about the same time in Constance Rourke's *American Humor*—acts stockly outrageous in his tough-guy bombast, gross eating, and callous violence.[4] West's carricature is more anxious than funny. The "roarer" smashes an Indian, catches Lem in a beartrap, and rapes Betty—all as responses to pioneer-style hospitality. The author's slapstick narrative violence seems as crude as the disdained Americana.

West's vehement negation of trite American cultural affirmations—an ideology especially promoted in the 1930s (though not taking a major academic role until the 1940s)—remains trapped in triteness. Inverted clichés, as George Orwell used to point out in defending honest use of language, remain clichés. But West often does not even invert them, apparently on the assumption that they can serve as their own self-mockery—an imitative fallacy. For example, when the battered Lem and the much abused Betty sit hungry and sad in Central Park, the narrator's comment is that they "felt a little better together because misery loves company." So do American clichés, however angry and disgusted one may be with them.

The Ivy League, and vanguardist, disdain for sleazy vulgarity also apparently includes fascination with it. Some of West's more arty efforts in *A Cool Million* concern whorehouse costuming, first in a burlesque of sophisticated "international styles" of the 1920s, then with a mockery of the sophistical Americana of the 1930s. For example: "Princess Roan Fawn from Two Forks,

Oklahoma Indian Reservation . . ." provided service with "baked
dog and fire-water" in a room "papered with birch bark to make
it look like a wigwam and she did business on the floor. Except
for a necklace of wolf's teeth, she was naked under her bull's-eye
blanket." The detailing is confused, coarsely mock-specific, with a
rather sniggering tone.

The author of *Balso Snell* remains no less disdainful of more
literary pretensions. One of the con men Lemuel becomes involved
with is "Sylvanus Snodgrasse, a poet both by vocation and avoca-
tion." He appears ready to put his bardic talents to work on our
Horatio Alger hero: "Poor Boy, Flying Team, Banker's Daughter . . . it's in the real American tradition and perfectly fitted to my
native lyre. Fie on your sickly Prousts, U.S. poets must write about
the U.S." This runs off into a pastiche mockery of heroic bombast,
of the usual academic literary criticism nonsense ("the horse
motif," symbolism, fancy allusions), and of cultural claims as a
cover-up for fraud (Snodgrasse is holding a crowd with his pseudo-
poeticizing in order for pickpockets to work it—and he robs "our
hero" as well).

Poet Snodgrasse appears again near the end of the fiction as
impressario of a traveling show, the "Chamber of American
Horrors, Animate and Inanimate Hideosities," which is also a cover
for propaganda work by international Communists. Snodgrasse,
the obtuse narrator informs us, "had become one of their agents
because of his inability to sell his 'poems.' " He, like many others,
"blamed his literary failure on the American public instead of his
own lack of talent, and his desire for revolution was really a
desire for revenge. Furthermore, having lost faith in himself, he
thought it his duty to undermine the nation's faith in itself." As
that last sentence indicates, this is a deadpan mockery of the philis-
tine view of literary-leftism of the early 1930s. Yet, since Snodgrasse
is also a shoddy crook and con man, West's response to the writer's
view of political engagement in the 1930s may be more ambiguous
than the topical satire intended.[5]

Among the inanimate horrors over which the con man-poet-
Communist presides are ersatz materials (imitation "wood"),

degraded art (a plaster "Venus de Milo with a clock in her abdomen"), gross ad-objects ("a gigantic hemorrhoid that was lit from within" by throbbing lights), cutesy double-purpose knick-nacks (a glass revolver "that held candy"), and the like. While this may have little to do with the Horatio Alger parody, West repeatedly expresses his repulsion, central to the modernist design and literary aesthetic, at the corrupted materials, fake form, and impure function. We see that a crucial Westean motive, even in a political work, remains aesthetic anger.

The show of hideosities in which Shagpoke and Lem perform also reportedly contains skits on the theme of "The Pageant of America or A Curse on Columbus," parodying pop history. These animatedly present our long record of exploitation, brutality, and genocide. Yet, in the rather too skittish manner which marks so much of this fiction, the uncomprehending narrator comments on the poet's linking the phony design and the brutal exploitation that the "arguments were not very convincing." But we do not hear the arguments, in spite of West's profound sense that American aesthetic and moral disorders are one: bad taste is ultimately bad politics. But so is bad writing.

The carnival sequence concludes with a crudely melodramatic playlet in which a grandmother and orphan children are cheated by salesmen become millionaires with phony bonds and then callously left to die in the streets. The manner does not get beyond old clichés about widows and orphans as victims of the capitalist system and is at least as crude as in West's "proletarian novel" contemporaries. The informing spirit is more depression outrage than irony on the gospel of success.

Perhaps West's harshest rhetoric on America as a phony civilization came earlier with a daubed-in figure, Israel Satinpenny, a Harvard educated militant Indian chief, who makes a two-page speech denouncing "white man's civilization." Not only have the whites destroyed the natural world, they have filled it with "syphillis and the radio, tuberculosis and the cinema," and other "surfeit of shoddy." In a takeoff on an apocalyptic biblical passage and 1930s images of consumerism, the chief says that the

white man used "all the powers of water, air and earth" to "turn his
wheels within wheels within wheels." "They turned, sure enough,
and the land was flooded with toilet paper, painted boxes to keep
pins in, key rings, watch fobs, leatherette satchels." All now becomes "refuse" and industrial-commercial "vomit." The rhetoric
slips into sophistication at odds with the style of the rest of the
novel, as when the Indian chief says, "Don't mistake me, Indians.
I'm no Rousseauistic philosopher. I know that you can't put the
clock back. But there is one thing you can do ... You can smash
that clock." That new "war cry," however, seems gratuitous since
the Indians "accepted" the dominant civilization that has now
"begun to doubt itself"; the white man's "final gift to us is
doubt, a soul-corroding doubt. He rotted this land in the name
of progress, and now it is he himself who is rotting." Apparently,
our civilizational self-hatred, as suggested by Spengler and Valery,
can only produce a revolt of synthetic Indians with a forced-draft
ideology which results in comic book violence. The manner here
is an on-and-off jokiness. Incidentally, as it were, Lemuel Pitkin
is scalped along the way, but so, indeed, may be the reader by the
rough edges of the fiction.

Depressing Politics

The suggestive stuff of *A Cool Million* lacks coherence and subtle
development. What shape the work has must be related to its
negative depression-era political concerns. And that is mostly the
nativist fascism around Shagpoke Whipple. This ex-president, who
exploitatively lent our hero a pittance on the family cow and
provided him with some of the more pernicious adages of American folk wisdom, meets up again with Lemuel in prison where,
according to his account, he was sent by the "two archenemies
of the American Spirit ... Wall Street and the Communists."
(The "Jewish international bankers," of course, have also been
in on it.) But true-gilt American, he will rise again because "this
is still the golden land of opportunity." Shagpoke and Lemuel

rejoin, bumming on the streets of New York, where Shagpoke's Panglossian Americanism has taken a more vicious turn. He has given up the Democratic party because of its "rank socialism" which would "take from American citizens their inalienable birthright; the right to sell their labor and their children's labor without restrictions as to either price or hours." This seems more literal quotation than satire (as I recall the words of a Christian minister and a schoolteacher who enlisted me as a child-crusader against "dictator wages" in the mid-1930s), though this may now seem comic bigotry directed against the New Deal capitalism-saving mild reforms of child-labor laws and minimum wages. (Of course we still seem to have some such antique rightists around.)

Shagpoke plans to counter "rank socialism" with the militant statism of a new National Revolutionary Party, popularly known as the "Leather Shirts." Its "Storm Troopers" will wear deerskin shirts and coonskin caps, and carry squirrel rifles. General Whipple proceeds to harangue vagrants around the Salvation Army with patriotic slogans and denunciations of "Jewish international bankers" and "Bolshevik labor unions." The Nazis, and such American off-shoots of the time as Pelly's Silver Shirts and Gerald L. K. Smith, provide West's rough model here. And though West has mocked the cultural ideology embraced by the political left in this period (folk-identifications, Americana, nativist literary traditions), his political analysis follows the popular Marxist view of fascism in that time. Thus Shagpoke attacks a supposed conspiracy of *large* capitalism and labor unions to appeal to the petty and *lumpen* bourgeois; as his rhetoric has it, "the small farmers and storekeepers, the clerks and petty officials" (and, as we see later, resentful nativist groups)—the "revolutionary middle class." While there may have been a partial social truth to this characterization of the mass base of fascism, it should be noted that it was also dubiously doctrinaire in refusing to acknowledge the authoritarian-chauvinistic appeal to, and support of, the "proletariate" (and other groups). The illiberality, "patriotism," broad repressiveness, and authoritarian longings of much of the "working class" has been evident through two world wars, the American social strife of the 1960s, and elsewhere, yet is usually denied in Marxist-tinged views. West, I will have occasion to note, carefully persisted in the stock-leftist view in the riot scene in his last novel, *The Day of the Locust*. His politics in both, then, though not his cultural views, were those identified as "Popular Front" in the 1930s.

Shagpoke's fascist-front campaign quickly turns into a comic-strip farrago as his rally is assaulted by limousine-delivered thugs brought in by a double-agent (a fat man in a Chesterfield coat) working for the Jewish bankers and the Russian secret police. In the episodic narrative, Shagpoke and Lem are separated, rejoin to operate an Indian follower's gold mine in order to finance the National Revolutionary Party, get violently separated again, and reunite to work for Snodgrasse's horror show. In the naturally fascist South, Shagpoke incites a lynch mob and racist riot. The violence appears mechanical, only motivated in stereotyped ways, and obsessional.

Lem, again separated during the riot from his ideological master, Shagpoke, eventually ends back in New York, ragged and emaciated but hardly outstanding "in the great army of unemployed" of the time. Extending the depression irony, Lemuel gets a job because of his crippled condition—another unemployed man has to be restrained from blinding himself to qualify. The job consists of serving as stooge for a vaudeville comic team, Riley and Robins (almost all figures in the novel appear in stock ethnic terms, a forerunner of later "sick" humor). The comics repeatedly beat Lem in a drearily slapstick routine; the cruel guffaws depend on his false teeth, glass eye, and artificial leg, uncontrollably and repeatedly flying off: "Fifteen Minutes of Furious Fun with Belly Laffs Galore." The innocent's violent dismantling has become his vocation and sole way of life. West's effects here might be described as sadistic-pathos, in an oddly fascinated repulsion with pathetic sadism.

The burlesque fiction of a burlesque show culminates in political prophecy. On Shagpoke Whipple's orders, as preparation for a

National Revolutionary Party takeover of New York City, Lemuel appears on stage in the American Storm Trooper "Leather Shirt" uniform to make an inciting speech. "I am a clown . . . but there are times when even clowns must grow serious. This is such a time. I"—and at that moment he is "drilled through the heart by an assassin's bullet," fired by the caricature double-agent of the international Jewish bankers and the Communist secret police in the Bijou theater. (Is there a displaced self-pity here for an anguished would-be comic writer?)

As the brief epilogue suggests, Lemuel Pitkin's dismantling and death were not in vain. The National Revolutionary Party, now in control of America, celebrates "Pitkin's Birthday" as a national holiday, with a parade of a hundred thousand coonskin capped youths down Fifth Avenue. West sticks in a flat *Lemuel Pitkin Song*, I suppose in martyr-parody of the Nazi's Horst Wessel leider. In other political parallelism, Shagpoke Whipple addresses his troops on the life of Lemuel Pitkin, a high "pilgrimage" in the "honorable tradition" of the all-American boy. Though he did not make his "fortune," and was violently dismantled and killed, he did finally succeed in the land of shoddy and blackened opportunity. For in "his martyrdom the National Revolutionary Party triumphed," delivering America "from sophistication, Marxism and International Capitalism." So: "All hail, the American Boy!"

Thus ends West's farcical treatment of the threat of American populist fascism. It is obviously a tract for the times, turning the Horatio Alger template, aesthetic disgust at the "surfeit of shoddy," obsessional concern with American violence, and despair at the Great Depression into an anxious fantasy of political outrage. But given the arbitrariness of the narrative and characterization, the trite thinness of the writing and detailing, the shoddy-on-shoddy tonalities, it is, even for those of us who also perceive much of America as fraudulent and violent, a forced metaphor with paranoic anxiety and anger loosely masquerading as political prophecy.[6]

West's Joke?

In one of his encounters with the mean legal system, Lemuel Pitkin desperately protests to a prosecuting attorney, "I'm innocent!" "So was Christ," sighingly notes the prosecutor, "and they nailed Him." Though here an incidental pun, the demolition (it is rather too broad to be properly called a "dismantling") of the all-American boy as sacrificial figure is in some ways consistent with the more serious "joke" of Christianity in *Miss Lonelyhearts*. All good intentions turn out to be hideously irrelevant. Virtue is fatal. Innocence gets nailed. Culture is a fraud, order a racket. All is consumed in pervasively gratuitous violence. But in *A Cool Million* few of the points are psychologically profound or paradoxically probing, just blatantly political.

Yet there may be another sense in which *A Cool Million* might be further understood as an involuted joke of Nathanael West's. The epigraph, which also provides the odd title, goes " 'John D. Rockefeller would give a cool million to have a stomach like yours.'—Old Saying." This perhaps points to the characteristic triviality at the end of the American fantasy of wealth and power. Rockefeller, also passingly mentioned in the narrative as a cynosure of success, may plausibly represent great acquisitiveness and hypocrisy combined with penuriousness and pettiness. Still, the epigraph and title only tangentially relate to the fiction. Perhaps, then, West also suggests that one indeed must have a strong stomach even to pretend to take in the cloying and cramping fantasies of American opportunity and success. He may also be suggesting a mocking perspective on the stomach-turning fraud and violence farcically played with in the narrative, as if to say, You, dear reader, must have an iron gut to tolerate Americana....

Neither reader nor writer can take such stuff as the American gospel of success, and its contingent clichés, with even satiric seriousness. *A Cool Million* is often compared to Voltaire's *Candide,* but the later work most essentially lacks the earlier one's detachment, "cool," in both detailing and pattern. Both attack simpleminded piety and gross optimism, but, in several senses, Voltaire had a "philosophical" control which the outraged American quite lacks. There was no escape for anxious Nathan from the all-consuming America, no distant contemplative garden to cultivate. For West, it was all a horrible joke, a nastily unpersuasive masquerade of maniacal greediness, vulgarity, hatred, and violence. It made him raging, nauseous, and anxious. West, though pretending a Perelman comic stance, had insufficient comic distancing; America was too painful to allow its ambivalently marginal son the play of possibility and wit.

West's partly earnest prophecy of populist fascism reveals some of the same outraged innocence which ostensibly is under attack in *A Cool Million.* Quite possibly populist fascism can happen here, with one of our recurrent cycles of "fundamentalist" moralism, vicious traditional piety, chauvinistic lashing out, and other politics of resentment curiously mislabeled "conservativism." Still, a more skeptical intelligence might well recognize, as we can retrospectively see so far, that American authoritarianism often develops more ambiguously, more "positively," and often under "liberal" guises and antiauthoritarian claims, as with "Wilsonian democracy," "New Deal" depression reforms, the World War II "Crusade" against totalitarianism, "Cold War anti-Communism," and other supposedly benevolent affirmations of not only Decency and Family ("Pro-Life") morality but of imperial internationalism and endless schooling indoctrination and, especially, technological progress. Perhaps the worst of all possible futures will fuse simple-minded righteousness with vast coercive power, costuming with old American moralism the endless technocracy.

But in his burlesque savaging of depression America, West did not allow very full play of ironic intelligence. *A Cool Million* may be seen as a psychodrama of the literalist political imagination. It might also be understood as a joke *on* its author. In rather righteously mocking the gross American costuming in innocence, West exposes his own innocence. He was outraged at the contradictory and fraudulent American culture and society, thus very Americanly denying part of its essence. The soured idealist misses his own ironies. Just as West's Lemuel achieves a horrible yet appropriate success, appropriate in its very grotesqueness—his martyrdom and idolatry for vicious purposes—so more generally with American faith. It works, in a sense, which is what is really wrong with it. Only a yearning innocent would confuse the shoddy fantasies of American opportunism and success with any concern for a just society and sensitive humaneness, and a meaningful future. The incomplete satirist revealed his own double bind. In his outraged disbelief, West believed too much in his stomach-turning America. Playing political moralist, he vomited forth less denial than allegiance. He, too, was bound to grotesquely and masqueradingly succeed, as perhaps only an American can.

Chapter Four

The Hollywood Masquerade:
The Day of the Locust

California Rococo Realism

Nathanael West's last and longest novel, *The Day of the Locust* (1939),[1] was apparently conceived in the mid-1930s, when he settled more or less permanently in Los Angeles as a script writer, and finished in 1938. Certainly the depression again influences the work, not only in the materials (unemployed actor become door-to-door salesman, two characters subsisting in a garage, a daughter whoring to pay the couple hundred dollars for her father's funeral, the artist happily turned studio hack for thirty dollars a week), but more generally in reinforcing West's ingrained pessimism. This applies to the politics, including the sense of possible "civil war" and West's continuation from his previous fiction of a partial leftist analysis of the feared petit bourgeois mob bitterly inclined to fascist demagoguery.

This emphasis on mass social realities, of course, is part of the depression era's pervasive turn to fictional techniques of "naturalism." While West's recorded comments indicate a strong distaste for Dreiserian, and related, novels, *Locust*, in fact, is much more "realistic" in manner than any of his other fictions. Indeed, the documentary impetus often seems dominant. West's careful mimicry of folk speech—with race-track tout Abe Kusich, unemployed bit-cowboy actor Earl Shoup, and would-be starlet Faye Greener—seems almost excessively reportorial. The bizarreness of the Hollywood materials, and the fanciful flourishes of some of West's metaphors and visual sense, should not be allowed to obscure the

67

reportorial insistence, the broad documentry emphasis, and, in sum, that *Locust* is in considerable part in the realistic mode.

While West's painterly eye and tropes (and perhaps a dozen allusions drawn from art history), take an important place in the fiction, the tone is less baroque and surreal than in *Miss Lonelyhearts*. In *Locust* art-emphasis also depends on considerable verisimilitude, both in character appropriateness—the central consciousness for much of the novel is a college educated painter working as a studio designer, Tod Hackett—and in reinforcing the heightened but still accurate descriptions of the southern California scenes.

While the opening description of the novel—ornately costumed Napoleonic soldiers, then "a little fat man" screaming through a megaphone, "Stage Nine, you bastards...!"—emphasizes incongruity, the disparity of prop and reality, it is a realistic one, even perhaps a literal one. Thus later in the first chapter, with the descriptions of the travesty decor of Los Angeles, such as the vulgarly romantic-imitation housing styles—"Mexican ranch houses, Samoan huts, Mediterranean villas, Egyptian and Japanese temples, Swiss chalets, Tudor cottages" (that last is still a highly popular, and grossly inappropriate, "style" in southern California housing tracts). Both studio and housing scenes emphasize "tasteless" ersatz romanticism for West's dominant concern with the sad comedy of the "truly monstrous" costuming of life, the masquerading, which is the ultimate American ordering.

Much of the grotesquery, that is, belongs to the time and place; West is less fancifully imagining than telling it as it was. He did, of course, write in an already well-worn subgenre of American documentry-exposé fiction, "the Hollywood novel." It went back several decades, and it was utilized in the 1930s by a number of noted writers (Dos Passos, Farrell, Cain, McCoy, O'Hara). F. Scott Fitzgerald, a friend of West's and also a script writer in this period, was working on his never completed (and not very good romantic-realistic Hollywood novel) *The Last Tycoon*. And many noted novelists (Huxley, Isherwood, Waugh, Mailer, Schulberg, Chandler, Hecht, MacDonald, Morris, Lurie) were to carry on the tradition. There was also a more vulgarly exploitative line of novels using Hollywood materials (Robbins, Carson, Block *et al*). Broadly considered in its subgenre, *The Day of the Locust* is not unusual in exposing the underside of "the dream factory" with an emphasis on the gross exploitation of romantic yearnings, the obsessional and somewhat perverse sexuality, and the contradictions of appearance and reality.[2]

What in the subgenre seems rather odd-angled in West's focus is the primary concern with the marginal. Where most Hollywood tales center on stars (the fantasy center) and producers (the power center), West, though describing some studio scenes and a briefly presented successful screen writer (Claude Estee) and one fancy decadent Hollywood party (stock for the form), mostly presents bit players, hangers-on, and the surrounding Angeleno crowd out of mid-America. West's Hollywood is largely that of the purlieus, that which more poignantly illustrates the psychological and social effects of the exploitative fantasy costuming of reality.

Not inappropriately, then, West makes the central consciousness of much of the novel a set and costume designer, Tod Hackett. However, he is only lightly backgrounded as a recent graduate of the "Yale School of Fine Arts" who has been rather fortuitously hired for the studio of National Films. Like his script-writing but serious novelist author, he makes his living by hack work but justifies himself by a different art culminating in the large prophetic (really anecdotal) painting he thinks about during the course of the novel, "The Burning of Los Angeles."

Some of the problems of the novel must be related to this figure who, in spite of the realistic manner, is little realized. We know more of lesser figures—Homer, Harry, Faye—than of the supposedly central one who functions mostly as a passive and voyeuristic auditor (a too-thin Nick Carraway). His "talent" is asserted along with the contradictory appearance of being "almost doltish." The author adds that underneath this was "really a very complicated young man, with a whole set of personalities . . . like a nest of Chinese boxes." But this West does not dramatize. Tod's one given inner box of serious painting exists mostly at the fantasy level— we little see him as a working and living painter—which may be an unintentional irony reinforcing the theme of fantasy role-playing.

It may often seem hard to take West's Tod with the seriousness the pattern of the work demands.[3] In spite of some private sensitivities and prophetic-artist identifications, he seems thinly—and a bit pretentiously—intellectual, a somewhat genteel slumming snob, the stock Ivy League dope. West, still partly trapped in one of his own earlier masquerades, did not clearly recognize the fatuousness. Though more self-conscious than the other hangers-on, Tod is similarly parasitic: sexually obsessed with the same auto-erotic adolescent girl, full of fantasies of violence and glory, and in the end simply another hysterical victim. Apparently West again wanted a double-viewed central figure, both profound and pathological, as in *Miss Lonelyhearts*—an intellectually perceptive artist and yet a victim of Hollywood fantasies. But they fail to fuse persuasively.

Certainly a number of Hollywood intellectuals, in the 1930s and later, thought of themselves as such paradoxical figures. (So, of course, have and do people in advertising, television, pop-magazine writing, and other exploitative careerism, including teachers who dream of writing a best-seller.) They live by, and rather thoroughly in, the processing of shoddy fantasies yet also claim to be above and beyond them as authentic artists and social moralists. So did Nathanael West. I think the preponderant evidence on such ambivalence supports the suspicion much voiced at that time (and mentioned in *Locust*) that they had "sold out," often far more than they knew. It is in the twentieth century the *trahison des clercs*. One catch is, to use a 1930s metaphor, "To sell corn, you have to have corn." And to have corn, you must have traded an essential part of humane intelligence. That was and is the price of adaptive American success. The media exploiters (as one can find in the written record as well as in personal experience) considerably believe, as they must, in what they are doing, as do most "successful" people. But exploitation and authenticity can rarely reside together for long.

Before, during, and after writing *The Day of the Locust*, Nathanael West was fully ensconced in lucrative but ugly and false

Hollywood script production. Personally as well as intellectually, he understood much of the consuming power and price of masquerading—the theme of the novel. So he needed to make his intellectual artist a Hollywood victim in sensibility, his serious prophetic painter a doltish Hollywood hack and parasite. It does not really work. As I will argue in several ways, *The Day of the Locust* may be understood as even more vengeantly "realistic" than intended. The conception and ironies turn back on themselves, the masquerading self-revealing and self-condemning.

The Greener Masquerading

Early in the novel, West makes a distinction between the "masqueraders," the costumed role-players characteristic of Hollywood (and, more generally, of the manipulative, shifting, and anomic southern California culture and society), and those retirees and other refugees, mostly from mid-America, who have "come to California to die," They, representing the broader American society, provide the audience of the masqueraders. Several things, as we will see, go novelistically wrong with this division, but let us first consider the Greeners, Harry and Faye, as epitomizing the masqueraders.

Harry is a clown. Clowning often serves as a combination of the self-protective and the self-punitive masquerade (as we often recognize in the adolescent "class clown"). But clowning can become compulsive, the masquerade turning into an entrapping mechanism.[4] West dramatized some of this with Beagle Darwin and Willie Shrike in his first two books and again in *Locust* with his most carefully detailed clown, Harry Greener, aging ex-vaudevillean, burlesque stooge, and sometime Hollywood bit player who makes his depression living huckstering with phony acts door-to-door a dubious homemade silver polish. "When Harry had first begun his stage career," forty years before, ruminates Tod, "he had probably restricted his clowning to the boards, but now he clowned continuously. It was his sole method of defense. Most people, he had discovered, won't go out of their way to punish a clown." His most successful professional role had been as a "bedraggled Harlequin" taking punishment from a group of acrobats (partly like Lem in the final scenes of *A Cool Million* playing masochistic stooge for the audience's sadistic guffaws). Now Harry specializes in burlesque pitifulness, playing the victim whenever he is "on," and overplaying the reverse, the rather nasty wise guy, when supposedly not masquerading. He dramatizes himself as the give-away fake, "dressing like a banker, a cheap unconvincing imitation" which by fooling no one "slyly" fools his auditors into sympathy. The "act" has become automatic.

Tod realizes this when in sickroom conversation Harry starts one of his compulsive routines and the auditor has "to let him run down like a clock." Though Harry's illness is "real," a heart attack which will shortly kill him, he "groaned skillfully. It was a second-act curtain groan, so phony that Tod had to hide a smile. And yet the old man's pallor hadn't come from a box." The only way Harry knows to express suffering is by exaggeratedly pretending it. His face, grotesquely overdone "like a mask" from the ravages of years of overacting, can never "express anything either subtly or exactly ... only the furthest degree." (Historically, it has become unfashionable in fictions as well as in life to find revelations of character in physiognomy or illness, but West repeatedly points to the old existential truth that we really are what we have done and do, not least the counterfeiting.) Harry's once-chosen role as victim has also fixated the pleasure in his suffering, though, of course, "he only enjoyed the sort that was self-inflicted." Harry inflicts on any and every one his life story, an unstoppable jokey-piteous charade of doggerel, mimicry, melodrama, bombast, and self-parodying comic patter. Hamming up his life has, in fact, become his life.

Earlier, we see him peddling his misery act and polish when (at Homer's house) he has a real heart attack. He acts hurt, and does hurt, "wondering himself whether he was acting or sick." The high point of his routine is his "victim's laugh" which he uses to victimize others. His intended sales victim (Homer) tries to stop Harry:

But Harry couldn't stop. He was really sick. The last block that held him poised over the runway of self-pity had been knocked away and he was sliding down the chute. . . . He jumped to his feet and began doing Harry Greener, poor Harry, honest Harry. . . . At the end of the pantomime, Harry stood with his head thrown back, clutching his throat as though waiting for the curtain. . . . But Harry wasn't finished. He bowed, sweeping his hat to his heart, then began again. He didn't get very far this time and had to gasp painfully for breath. Suddenly, like a mechanical toy that had been overwound, something snapped inside him and he began to spin through his entire repertoire. The effort was purely muscular, like the dance of a paralytic. He jigged, juggled his hat, made believe he had been kicked. . . . He went through it all in one dizzy spasm, then reeled to the couch. . . .

As real victim he was "even more surprised" than his ostensible victim-audience; though "really sick," he can only think and re-spond in terms of "performance." While playing faint, he shock-ingly discovers that he really "is faint." Having role-played so much, he can no longer tell when his is acting pain and feeling pain, pretending suffering and really suffering. In role-playing desperation, like the poseur-poet in *Balso Snell*, his posing act takes over on its frenziedly mechanical own. The masquerade has become all.

The narrator's (and author's) detailed fascination with the Greener role-playing may be because Harry is a genuine fake, all pose with little person left over. So, too, with his daughter, Faye Greener, central idol in most of the violent masquerade of West's mock-scenario of Hollywood eroticism. From the second chapter to concluding riot-rehearsal, Faye is the unmoved mover of the obsessional sexual fantasies of all the particularized males in the novel. An unloving parody love goddess, she provides another masturbatory rape image of the long-dominant Hollywood fantasy type (Harlowe, Monroe, et al). A pretty would-be starlet, tall ("with sword-like legs"), wide chested and high breasted, "plat-inum" blonde seventeen year old (she usually looks even younger), she is "taut and vibrant" with a constant sexual come-on. Analyz-ing his own longings for Faye, Tod realizes her appeal "wasn't

to pleasure" but to something else, "closer to murder than to love."
In further images, coupling with Faye becomes an act of mindless
self-immolation, an almost inverted mystical experience, which is
much of what media eroticism is about. Even doltishly passive
Tod has repeated visions of raping Faye.[5]

The erotic deity is peurile and mannered, with a "subtle half-
smile uncontaminated by thought," sexual fantasy unencumbered
by other human dimensions. Her compulsive sexual gestures were
"so completely meaningless, almost formal, that she seemed like
a dancer rather than an affected actress," which she was badly
imitating. Much of the time she mechanically, self-lovingly, pos-
tures before mirrors. Even to tasteful Yalie Tod, her "affectations"
were "so completely artificial that he found them charming." Like
Harry's, Fay's role-playing works by not fooling anyone; instead,
it was "like being backstage during an amateurish, ridiculous play."
The very totality of her absurdity takes people in, with a knowing
smile but none the less caught. For example, we several times
see one of her "most characteristic gestures" of erotic signaling
"with a secret smile and the tongue caress" of her parted lips:
"It seemed to promise all sorts of undefined intimacies, yet it was
really as simple and automatic as the word thanks." But that very
impersonality, the unencumbered sexual come-on, is the appeal.

Faye constantly turns and twists her well-shaped body in sexual
automation. Even the sophisticatedly blasé screenwriter, Claude,
is mesmerized by it. He eagerly listens to her expound on Hollywood as she jumbles "bits of badly understood advice from the
trade papers . . . fan magazines and . . . legends"—all "nonsense"—
but, like most of her auditors, he is "busy watching her smile,
laugh, shiver, whisper, grow indignant, cross and uncross her
legs, stick out her tongue, widen and narrow her eyes, toss her
head. . . ." It is a weirdly dissociated performance of gestures and
words. Like other perhaps sincerely fraudulent people (Richard
Nixon provides a famous example), her body language disconnects
from her words, "her gestures and expressions didn't really illus-
trate what she was saying. They were almost pure. It was as
though her body recognized how foolish her words were. . . ." But

most of the listeners are not really connecting with her body, but with the fantasy of using it. Faye, an automated sexual charade, is as bad an actress otherwise as most popular media figures, existing only as crude fantasy image.

And that does express her. She lives in fantasy. In a scene of careful dramatization, West shows her choosing her "stories," running through stock fantasies as if thumbing a deck of cards. She takes them earnestly, wholeheartedly, sincerely stupid and ungenuine, proposing to friend Tod, whom she uses but never sexually, various garbled but literal-minded "B" movie scripts of the time—"a South Sea tale," a "familiar version of the Cinderella theme"—as something that would make them successful and rich. As so often in *Locust*, Tod summarizes the quality in a painting analogy: "Although the events she described were miraculous, her description of them was realistic. The effect was similar to that obtained by the artists of the Middle Ages, who, when doing a subject like the raising of Lazarus from the dead or Christ walking on water, were careful to keep all the details intensely realistic." (So does West with his fantasy figures.) Faye's literalism thus achieves a naive power. And a deeper irony since her faith is not cosmic Christianity but Hollywood shoddy, the crassest commercial-romantic junk, in which she is a true believer, an erotic nun of masturbatory dreams. It is "these little daydreams of hers" which "gave such extraordinary color and mystery to her movements," a tumescent holiness total in its human counterfeit. Faye is a mystical vibrating machine. And it seems to be this autoeroticism which leads to the male audiences' rape-longings against her mad "completeness, egg-like self-sufficiency," that makes even Tod "want to crush her," or throw "her down in the soft, warm mud" of the fantasy swamp that she lives in. This is violating, as an old form of pornography emphasized, the nun, only this time of Hollywood fantasy-piety.

Faye's tormenting aroused males, fighting with her father (she counters his maniacal "victim's laugh" with mechanically lascivious singing of "Jeepers-Creepers"), or setting off violence between her incidental lovers (Earl, the drugstore cowboy, Miguel, the

Mexican cockfighting primitive), do not really affect her. Nor apparently does her complacent whoring. It cannot faze her, Tod concludes, because "her beauty was structural like a tree's, not a quality of her mind or heart." She is simply not a real person.

When Harry dies, Faye, who has been treating him meanly, decides to role-play, rather forcedly, the devoted daughter. She will provide a proper funeral. And for that, within a few paragraphs, her language switches from stock sentimentality to tough-broad slang as she plans to earn the funeral money on her back—call girl for Mrs. Jenning's high-class establishment. After all, it is just another role-playing. Indeed, when she takes on a role that bothers her, as does her chaste moving in with middle-aged Homer as a "business arrangement" to provide her with the clothes, convertible, and other fetish accoutrements that will certify her stardom, she finds the doggily devoted dope shame-arousing, and so decides to cancel the role. While Faye gets carefully delineated with touches of shame, anger, geniality, even lasciviousness, and a "viper" high (from the song she sings, earlier slang for a "stoner" or "pothead"), these can only be incidental to her masquerading, which is most of the essential self she has.

Tod's final vision of Faye, after the day of a gruesome and fraudulent cockfight in the garage and then a parallel stud fight in Homer's living room between Faye's sexually teased admirers, provides a metaphoric summary. He wonders if she has gone off with Miguel, whom she went to bed with the previous night, or, more likely, back to whoring for Mrs. Jenning:

But either way she would come out all right. Nothing could hurt her. She was like a cork. No matter how rough the sea got, she would go dancing over the same waves that sank iron ships and tore away piers of reinforced concrete. He pictured her riding a tremendous sea. Wave after wave reared its ton on ton of solid water and crashed down only to have her spin gaily away. . . . a pretty cork, gilt with a glittering fragment of mirror set in its top. The sea in which it danced was beautiful, green in the trough of the waves and silver at their tips. But for all their moondriven power, they could do no more than net the bright cork for a moment in a spume of intricate lace. Finally it was set down on a strange shore where a savage with pork-sausage fingers and a pimpled butt picked it up and hugged it to his sagging belly. Tod recognized the fortunate man; he was one of Mrs. Jenning's customers.

The passage serves to again reveal Tod's own passive fantasy indulgence, but it also does other things. In this vintage West, an extended conceit, we see the intentional yoking of incongruities— gilt cork and concrete pier, intricate lace and pimpled butt, lyrical nature poetry and crude human grotesquery, wild vision and hard-nosed cynicism. But the larger significance may be seen in the final judgment of Faye-as-cork: narcissistic (the fragment of mirror on top), partially exempt from the natural order in her very denaturing (uncapturable by the destructive sea), subject only to one of her parodistic South Sea romance scripts, turned back into properly whorish reality. Faye, as person and type, is invulnerable, not only in her metaphoric journey here but in her "life" in the novel as well as in her final symbolism as a figure in Tod's painting, "The Burning of Los Angeles" (running ecstatically ahead of the ravaging locust-mob, who revengefully pursue the masqueraders who have helped cheat them of genuine life).

Faye is unfazable. But that also means she floats invulnerable to most human possibilities, always in bouncing escape, only momentarily netted in the spume. Neither tragic nor comic, Faye remains unarousable to fuller life, just a dancing cork in a kaleidoscopic masquerade of autoeroticism. Though bemused in tone, the passage may be read as propounding West's devastating view of the consequences of endless role-playing. With Faye always bouncing free to continue in her fantasies, or Harry not knowing what he feels because clownishly playing his disguised self, the Greeners show that for compulsive masqueraders little authentic life is possible. It is a disease of unreality as bad as religion. What "Hollywood" means, then, is not just the obvious grossness and corruption but the "greener" fantasy masquerading of life and self—and all America.

West's compassionate handling of the Greeners, and indeed of the whole masquerading ambience, should not detract from the sense of horror. Here, as he wrote in *Miss Lonelyhearts*, we can see some of the great "betrayal" of human dreams. Since West's time, our exploitative technocratic popular culture has extended, increased, and intensified; larger realms of daily activities—politics, religion, schooling, social responses, culture—have more fully merged into the masquerades. The probabilities can hardly be less than apocalyptic.

Machined Fantasies

Though not much of *The Day of the Locust* concerns cinema production, West seems to have perceived that an essence of the Hollywood "art" was to provide mechanical fantasies of violent eroticism for repressed mass America. His imagery for Los Angeles insists strongly on machined fantasy, fabricated dreams which become grotesque monstrosities. So, too, with his often wryly amusing descriptions of his caricature people. For example, Earl Shoup, Faye's stud and a minor cowboy actor, costumed in Western clothes, gestures, and clichés, "had a two dimensional face that a talented child might have drawn with a ruler and a compass." The flat symmetry of features and the coloring like a wash "completed his resemblance to a mechanical drawing." A mechanical and two-dimensional persona, his responses, mostly laconic posing and sex and violence, lack most fuller human depth.

Throughout the fiction, West plays variations on the mechanical phantasm. Tod goes to a party at the imitation Mississippi mansion in Los Angeles of successful screen writer Claude. His host has made masquerading into an infinite regress of mockery, such as calling to his butler, " 'Here you black rascal! A mint julep.' A Chinese servant came running with a Scotch and soda." A more simple mechanism, a floodlighted "conversation piece" (as it was later to be called by similar affluently bored people), is a "dead horse" in his swimming pool, "or, rather, a life-size, realistic reproduction of one. Its legs stuck up stiff and straight and it had an enormous, distended belly. Its hammerhead lay twisted to one side and from its mouth, which was set in an agonized grin, hung a heavy black tongue." Why is this grotesque mechanism there? "To amuse."

Claude also jokes with a parody rhetoric "that permitted him to express his moral indignation and still keep his reputation for worldliness and wit." So did Nathanael West, and other characters in his fiction such as "joke machine" Shrike, in a desperate effort to amuse, to mask horror and emptiness. Claude wants Tod to join the party in visiting Audrey Jenning's classy whorehouse to watch what turns out to be a blandly obscene movie of polymorphous sex. Tod demurs. Claude explains that the cultivated madam —"refined," she "insists on discussing Gertrude Stein and Juan Gris"—"makes vice attractive by skillful packaging. Her dive's a triumph of industrial design." "I don't care how much cellophane she wraps it in," Tod counters, "nautch joints are depressing, like all places for deposit, banks, mail boxes, tombs, vending machines." With cynical playfulness, Claude picks up the mechanical metaphor: "Love is like a vending machine, eh? Not bad. You insert a coin and press home the lever. There's some mechanical activity inside the bowels of the device. You receive a small sweet, frown at yourself in the dirty mirror, adjust your hat . . . and walk away, trying to look as though nothing had happened. It's good, but it's not for pictures." For instead of this mechanical autoeroticism, after all, the "barber in Purdue" wants an even more counterfeit mechanism of "amour and glamor." But all possibilities remain "industrial design."[6]

So does most of the southern California scene, including the fantasy ersatz ("plastic," people in the 1970s would say) styles of housing and decorating and costuming: sports clothes which were "really fancy dress"; imitation northern European cottages (Homer's is described in ugly detail) for a Mediterranean climate; plants made of "rubber and cork" mixed with real ones; everything painted and plastered and stamped to pretend to be something else (the "surfeit of shoddy" of *A Cool Million*, the violation of function and the nature of materials). By contagion, apparently, even nature appears as machined artifice. In truly apt metaphors, we get the night scene in Los Angeles in which, amid Claude's mimosa and oleander, through "a slit in the blue serge sky poked a grained moon that looked like an enormous bone button." That metaphoric direction had been set in the opening chapter with images of dusk with its semidesert purplish tones in which "violet piping, like a Neon tube, outlined the tops of the ugly, hump-backed hills." Much later in the story, it becomes "one of those blue and lavender nights when the luminous color seems to have been blown over the scene with an airbrush." The Westean twist to grotesquery almost convinces the reader that the hills are crippled and all the natural ambience tasteless machine work. Yet in comparison with the hard industrial and class impositions on nature in the East, it has crass charm.

West's stylistic problem is to find the metaphors which will meaningfully encompass the crippled beings within the mechanical artifice. He uses painting styles as analogues, in the first chapter having Tod announce his turn away from the positive Americana of Homer and Ryder for the sharper nineteenth-century European mockeries of Daumier and Goya. Somewhat after the middle of the novel, Tod favors the eighteenth-century picturesque painters of decay, such as Rosa and Guardi. Later, observing the Holly-wood cultists, he turns to the tortured mannerism of Magnasco. Tod's projected painting, "The Burning of Los Angeles," suggests a combination of Ensor's early twentieth-century apocalyptic sym-bolism, surrealist incongruities (as do the machined nature de-scriptions quoted above)—and perhaps rather too much disaster-epic illustration, Hollywood style, since popular culture usually shows an exploitative willingness to mask cheap sensationalism and emptiness as portentous apocalypse.

An obvious part of the machined-fantasy conception comes out in the prop versus reality studio scenes where the mechanisms, and false facades, of dreams are so evident. The studio backlot serves as a "dream dump" for discarded sets and props. It is compared to T. A. Janvier's [In the] Sargasso Sea (a novel [1898] drawing a mythic illustration of the mid-Atlantic doldrums which collect flotsam and jetsam—and in legend, the Flying Dutchman and the Ancient Mariner). The studio, then, is "a Sargasso of the imagination!" (The metaphor had been used earlier in Ezra Pound's satiric portrayal of a culture-vulture rich lady, "Portrait d'un Femme".) The Hollywood "dream dump" is where every fantasy will be exploited and washed up.

This includes the costuming of history as well. Returning (Chapter 18) to his opening studio scene of the filming of "The Battle of Waterloo," we get ironic play on defeat—for the historic Napoleon because of a collapsed cavalry charge at Mont St. Jean, for the movie production because of the collapsed (unfinished) wood-canvas-plaster set of Mont St. Jean. Real people get hurt in the collapse, though they express, depression style, pleasure at the likelihood of injury compensation. The traditional mock-heroic provides the method here: great event, shoddy mechanical imitation, practical human point.

But much of West's treatment develops from more direct realism than these highlighted allusions and metaphors would suggest. Simply presenting actual southern California scenes and types gives more than enough of the bizarre. Note, for example, a comic-gruesome set piece: Mrs. Loomis comes upon Tod and Homer while searching for her darling child, Adore, talks to Tod of California as a "paradise," of her faith in raw vegetables (following one "Dr. Pierce . . . 'Know-All Pierce-All' " in "the search for Health along the Road of Life"), and of her obsessional displaced ambitions to make her child a screen star (the widespread "Squirrely Temple" craze as it was sometimes called in the 1930s). Adore, an artificially manner little boy of eight, appears, "with a pale, peaked face and a large troubled forehead . . . staring eyes . . . eyebrows . . . plucked and shaped . . . dressed like a man." Already full of horrific psychological tics, he makes faces; his mother apologetically explains that she thinks he is the "Frankenstein monster"—and so he is! She forces her machine-fantasy monster-child to perform, "expertly" singing a semiobscene hyped-blues, "Mamma Doan Wan' No Peas," while imitatively writhing with "a top-heavy load of sexual pain." (Such grotesque role-playing, of course,

continues and expresses an all-American ideal of the "loving" ambitious parent, as with those tens of thousands of petit bourgeois
ones who drive their daughters to be competitive and posturing
baton twirlers, cheerleaders, fashion models, and other mechanically tuned and costumed obscenities, and their sons to be jocks.)
Not at all incidentally, Adore breaks through his imposed role
with inevitable violence, later throwing a stone at the near-
psychotic Homer, which starts the mass violence of the final riot
scene in the novel. West several times stresses the point that
the role-players, by the obvious psychological mechanisms of repression and release, turn nasty.

Not quite all the masqueraders come out as such inhuman
"automatons." Almost sarcastically, West presents as the most
naturally spontaneous and responsive a three-foot dwarf, "Honest Abe Kusich," racetrack tout, pugnacious friend of whores and
Tod, earnest handler of the losing bird in the rigged cockfight,
and crusher of Earl's testicles when monopolizing Faye's atten-
tions at the following party. Indomitable midget, Abe masquerades
as a big macho tough guy, and in a not altogether ironic sense
really is. But West, with a natural taste for the grotesque (as
Balso Snell in his first fiction had a taste for cripples), perhaps expands too much on the role-playing of the dwarf, of Harry Greener,
and of other grotesqueries such as a satire of a performing trans-
vestite (a man who badly imitates a man). The author performs
rather too much as transfixed Eastern aesthete with the Southland
decor. Some of this, of course, may be attributed to writing in the
rather documentary form of the "Hollywood novel" and its emphasis on bizarre detail. Postsick and black humor, which it fore-
shadows, it may have lost some of its shock and comic effects. But
perhaps more generally West's fiction can be taken as implying
what was to happen: the machined fantasies represented by Hollywood in an earlier period were to invade the repressed American
character. But the result was to be less the violent upheaval with
which West concludes his story than the Hollywoodization of
everything until an amorphous counterfeit culture provided a technocratic masquerade of a civilization.

The Death-Longing Middle Americans

As noted earlier, West sets up, as both subject of his prophetic painting and as human topography of southern California, two looming types: the "masqueraders" (Harry, Faye, Claude—and the people at his party—Tod, Earl, Abe, and, more generally, all the role-players); and those "who came to California to die," the embittered and repressed middle-western refugees from an older American order. West's dichotmizing here gets the fiction in several kinds of trouble. The point of view becomes unprofitably split. For the first seven chapters it hovers around Tod who, whatever his inadequacies, shows some reflective ability in terms of his painter's visual analysis, his self-ironies about his sexual obsession with Faye, and his other social and historical awareness. Tod at least partly can carry Westean self-conscious intelligence. But then the point of view switches for six chapters, hovering around Homer Simpson, truly doltish and a psychological "automaton," who cannot coherently carry much perception or thought. Then, to regain momentum and intelligence—and to return to the essential painting analogues and ironic-apocalyptic vision—the focus moves back to Tod for the remainder of the story. Initially, Homer represents those who came to die, as against the masqueraders. He is a just arrived middle-aged ex-hotel bookkeeper from Waynesville, Iowa, convalescing from psychophysical illness and seeking escape from his psychological crippling—a pathetic victim of near-total sexual repression, a drastically restricted life, and a fearfully deadened sensibility.

But the confusion in the novel enlarges with the contradictory treatment of Homer. While it seems evident that West wanted to center on Homer to dramatize the nonmasqueraders—he is the only one substantially individualized—and to probe those who form the actual mob at the concluding premiere, the symbolic mob of Tod's "The Burning of Los Angeles," and the potential (and politically threatening) mob of "locusts" of the Book of Revelation prepared to ravish the land as the portent of the end of time, Homer turns into a semimasquerader. Clearly in Tod's painting,

Homer runs with the masqueraders (Faye, Harry, Claude, and Tod), though somnambulistically almost falling out of the picture. Iconographically, as well as dramatically, he is not one of his fellow middle-American refugees but their victim. Also by switch of narrative focus, Tod, West, and the reader, have come to sympathetically identify with Homer. True, he has painfully fallen in love with Faye (after meeting her because of Harry's fortuitous illness at Homer's house), become exploitatively involved in her masquerade as a "star," and through Faye becomes friendly with Tod and involved with Earl and others. Faye even forces him out of his gray suits and into colorful California costuming and partying, though these are nauseatingly inappropriate to Homer (and treated with Ivy League scorn by West). But every one recognizes the painfully imposed roles, and Homer remains a nonmasquerader.[7]

When Faye's mistreatment of the lovingly masochistic dummy culminates in a mock orgy and mock riot at Homer's house, she ends up in bed with Miguel. Homer hears her moaning in orgasm and uncomprehendingly comes in to bring her an aspirin. Faye and her two studs flee. Homer breaks down into psychosis, a victim of the Greener masquerading, not a masquerader.

Homer has been several ways dramatized as anything but a role-player. A smalltown hotel bookkeeper, he left Iowa in desperation, fallen ill after almost having sex with an alcoholic woman who offers him that compensation for an overdue hotel bill. That was one of the very few events in his emptily accounting twenty years of "working ten hours, eating two, sleeping the rest." Even when this somnambulist struggles to semiwakefulness, his body betrays him—"He got out of bed in sections, like a poorly made automaton...." Elsewhere he is compared to a sleepwalker, a blind man, and a broken machine. His hands, in one of West's playfully elaborate metaphoric extensions, also betray him; sometimes asleep when the rest of him is awake, he must carry them to a basin of cold water, where they behave on their own "like a pair of strange aquatic animals." Accidentally meeting Faye, Homer remains submissively withdrawn, but his hands are aroused, itch, then become "hot and swollen." After Faye leaves, the hands "trembled and jerked, as though troubled by dreams," which Homer never knowingly is, and so he clasps them together. But they give him away again, twining "like a tangle of thighs in miniature. He snatched them apart and sat on them." Elsewhere, his hands also seemed to show "a life and will of their own," the only naturally responsive part of him.

When Homer starts going to pieces at the brawl over Faye's nasty treatment of him and sexual come-on to all the other men, his hands go into the compulsive ritualism of a "manual ballet," doing the childish pattern of here's the church here's the steeple, then cracking all their joints one by one, a total round which he always does three times, between alternate trappings in armpits, under thighs, between knees. This compulsive hand-ritual—perhaps indebted to the somewhat less grotesque one of Wing Biddlebaum, the repressed homosexual outcast school teacher in Sherwood Anderson's *Winesburg, Ohio* (some similar tics also appear in Dickens)—must be one of the most elaborate masturbatory displacements ever recorded in fiction.[8]

Other than with his hands, Homer is usually close to psychic paralysis. Curiously, in one metaphor Homer's emotions are compared to a rearing wave—like the one that bounces invulnerable Faye in Tod's final vision of her—yet for Homer the wave never crashed, just "collapsed to run back like water down a drain, leaving . . . only the refuse of feeling." His strongest direct responses include happily identifying with a fly that escapes the lizard by his garbage can, moments of paranoia in the street, and trembling before Faye's small brutalities. Totally repressed, this virginal middle-aged man turns chastity into "both spine and armor," like "the shell of a tortoise." And comments Tod, it must continue; sexual release would be explosively disintegrating—as its substitute violence becomes in the final mob scene. Homer can achieve little relief; to sing in his solitude, he does the only song he knew (in parody of the cultural poverty of middle-America), "The Star-Spangled Banner."[9] Homer can neither choose nor change, only sink in the sour sadness of an "anguish . . . basic and permanent." Or abase himself in "cringing, clumsy dog" servility with the divine Faye, which makes even usually invulnerable Faye feel a bit ashamed, therefore vulnerable, therefore nasty. Or Homer sobs in a totally hopeless way: "The sound was like an axe chopping pine, a heavy hollow, chunking, noise. It was repeated rhythmically but without accent. There was no progress in it. Each chunk was exactly like the one that preceded. It would never reach a climax."

West's mode here of frequently brilliant metaphors, however hyperbolic in pattern, achieves great poignancy from a compassionately disinterested (as against sentimental) pathos. He follows through with the catatonia that inevitably awaits a Homer. Tod finds him collapsed on the final day into a tight ball, "like a steel spring which has been freed of its function in a machine and allowed to use all its strength centripetally." This "original coil" reminds Tod of a picture in an abnormal psychology text of "uterine flight," about which he muses: "What a perfect escape the return to the womb was. Better by far than Religion or Art or the South Sea Islands. . . ." In psychotic withdrawal, then, we may again find the sardonic ultimate answer to Miss Lonelyhearts. Except, of course, that it, too, cannot work for outside exists a real world of gratuitous possibilities. Homer sleepwalkingly wanders from his womb-coil on the way back to Iowa, pajamas under his gray suit and sticking out of his opened fly, stonily oblivious to Tod and the crowd he has wandered into—another lonelyhearts scapegoat—except to Adore's stone in his face which sets him to murderous reaction. We last see his death-longing violent submergence in the mob. If Homer may be said to masquerade in his automaton somnambulism, masturbatory hands-compulsion, uterine flight, and self-destruction, it is only in an ultimate pathos of necessarily rejecting the human.

With a poetry less poignant—indeed, hostile unto paranoia— West only briefly annotated the rest of those who came to California to die. They are, in an early chapter, the unchanging audience of Tod's lithographs, "The Dancers," who antagonistically "stared at the masqueraders" and drove them "to spin crazily and leap into the air with twisted backs like hooked trout." (*Locust* displays a number of the late-West's hunting and fishing metaphors, adding an unexpected "natural" but still violent tone.) Performers and audience, here and elsewhere, remain symbiotic, the masqueraders merely the captive fish of the mob. I can only explain West's overemphatic reversal of the usual performer-audience and media-mass exploitative relations as some rather paranoid inversion by the guilty false-artist. However that may be, and however much the mob may really consist of pathetic Homers (and the lovelorn of West's earlier vision), the author now views them far more externally, socially, than in his early writing.

Toward the end of the novel Tod draws the devotees of Hollywood religion, "the 'Church of Christ, Physical' where holiness was attained through the constant use of chestweights and spring grips; the 'Church Invisible' where fortunes were told and the dead made to find lost objects; the 'Tabernacle of the Third Coming' where a woman in male clothing preached the 'Crusade Against Salt'; and the 'Temple Moderne' under whose glass and chromium roof 'Brain-Breathing, the Secret of the Aztecs' was taught." The level of mockery here seems scornfully distant, rather pat in its lack of sympathy or perplexity. Oddly, too, he sees the *California* worshippers as with "drained-out, feeble bodies" and "wild, disordered minds." This seems less actual than a depression-cum-fear rhetoric about an "awful, anarchic power" that could "destroy civilization." The one description of a ranting individual melodramatizes him with "countersunk eyes, like the heads of burnished spikes," as he might have been drawn by "Magnasco,"; the image does belong to an earlier time and seems imposed on 1930s Californians. West pushes hard with the figure: "The message that he brought to the city was one that an illiterate anchorite might have given decadent Rome. It was a crazy jumble of dietary rules, economics and Biblical threats. He claimed to have seen the Tiger of Wrath stalking the walls of the citadel and the Jackal of Lust skulking in the shrubbery, and he connected these omens with 'thirty dollars every Thursday' and meat eating." But this "messianic rage," which we are told sets off the congregation, seems not right to my ear, not only inconsistent with the documents of the period but with much of the rest of

West's portrayal of the mob—a Shrike-Greener-West rhetorical pose. The contemptuous allusions to the populist "Townsend
Plan" of the period (regular payments to the elderly from public funds) and to vegetarians, combine with a pretentious fear for
"civilization," and express the political paranoia that dominated
also *A Cool Million* and its overdone warning of the fascist mob.
West's "progressivism" (in those times often actually a very
conservative social ideology) seems to control the rhetoric and
twist the realities.[10]

Other brief touches about the mob character include the "expression of vicious, acrid boredom that trembled on the edge of
violence" from the strangers watching Harry's funeral. But in
spite of such progressive-paranoia, even Tod-West can be more
thoughtfully self-questioning: he "wondered if he weren't exaggerating the importance of the people who came to California to die," and concludes "they were only the pick of America's
madmen." Jumping metaphors, however, he decides that there
was enough violence in the national milk from which this "cream"
came that throughout the country there "would be civil war."
Granted, it may be easy hindsight for us to see this as a tritely
specious progressive piety and fear of the depression period.
Ironically, in context the ruminations arise not from populist violence but from Tod's own, his foiled desire to rape Faye, and his
somewhat ambivalent role-playing a Jeremiah artist. Here, as several other times in the novel, West confusingly imposes some of
the abstract politics of the alienated intellectuals of the time,
elitist conservative-progressive notions of the popular mob and of
social fear, violating his own poignant artistic perception of an
individual in and out of that mob, Homer.

Perhaps, then, West's political ideology pushed him to the
inconsistent, and sometimes inverted, masquerader-mob duality.
At times, I think, his art is too insightful to stay with his own
impositions. Thus Tod, thinking again of sexually assaulting Faye
while sitting, with masturbatory fantasy appropriateness, in the
dark of a movie theater, "began to wonder if he himself didn't
suffer from the ingrained, morbid apathy he liked to draw in

others." "Morbid apathy," not "messianic rage," seems the more likely real American mob emotion (and was essential to the technocracy to come). Tod adds, "Maybe he could only be galvinized into sensibility and that was why he was chasing Faye," true muse of the apathetic middle-American mob as well as of its masquerading artist.

Is This the Promised End?

That brings us to the final scene of *The Day of the Locust* (chapter 27) where a crowd of thousands gathers to see the celebrities at "the world premiere" of an unidentified movie at a famous Hollywood theater. It turns into a multiple riot, with the police covertly beating those they arrest, the crowd frenziedly surging, and Tod-West rather hysterically projecting its mood ("the crowd would turn demonic," "collectively it would grab and rend"). Some of the falsity gets wryly attributed to the media (a generation before that became a fashionable charge), such as a cynically manipulative radio reporter with an "hysterical voice." Tod, fortuitously caught up in the scene, gets threateningly treated until he plays along with the nasty humor of those around him.

West's analysis by way of Tod's commentary to himself is partly ideological, as with the nationalistic revolutionary mob in *A Cool Million*. He claims not to "see any working men. The crowd was made up of the lower middle classes. . . ." Surely this imposes on the reality. These furtive folk, he goes on, once become collective are threatening. No longer "harmless curiosity seekers," they reveal that "they were savage and bitter, especially the middle-aged and the old, and had been made so by boredom and disappointment." Except for the point about boredom, this shows the stock leftist view of the time about the fascist mob developing from the embitteredly anxious petit bourgeois. However, West's description seems contradictory: "All their lives they had slaved at some kind of dull, heavy labor, behind desks and counters, in the fields and at tedious machines of all sorts . . . dreaming of the leisure that would be theirs. . . ." So it is, after all, a partly working class mob. But West's concern really turns about cheated sensibility rather than economic class, in spite of his political bias of the times. Thus the euphoric promise of California has gone sour for those who "don't know what to do with their time. They haven't the mental equipment for leisure, the money or the physical equipment for pleasure." Not yet blessed with affluent technocracy's distractions, their "boredom becomes more and more terrible. They realize they've been tricked and burn with resentment." (I wonder if West's analysis would not be more persuasive if he had followed through with the rest of the middle Americans what he had dramatized with Homer— boredom as the result of repression, the denaturing anxiety from the puritanic denial of the sensual, the aesthetic, the free.) The popular media have directed mob-man's displaced emotions towards "lynchings, murder, sex crimes, explosions, wrecks, love nests [sic?], fires, miracles, revolution, war." The petit bourgeois masses, consequently, have sophisticated longings for extremity, but "nothing can ever be violent enough to make taut their slack minds and bodies. They have been cheated and betrayed." Here, as with the worst "betrayal" of common humanity in *Miss Lonelyhearts* (discussed in chapter 2), West again indicts the debased and exploited dreams, the fantasy masquerades of reality. The self-denaturing and self-defeating fantasies, personified by the masqueraders (such as the movie celebrities they have gathered together to see), backlash in an embittered emptiness and resentment which induces violence.

Their representative, Homer, fortuitously wanders into the crowd scene and ends up stomping the miniature masquerader, the mannequin-child Adore, who provokes him with a stone in the face. That dramatization of their own longing sets off the crowd in explosive turmoil. Tod, head bruised, ribs damaged, ankle broken, focuses several pages of intense description of mob behavior, including his harshly twisting a boy's neck to desperately free himself and smashing an old man in the head who sexually molests a young girl. The girl gets away but Tod sees another man grab her. West's description of a certain kind of mob action seems apt, including the dramatized dialogue of a momentary calm in which Tod finds people "enjoying themselves" in voyeuristic sexual sadism and in sexual advances in the press of bodies. When the crowd surges again, Tod saves himself by painfully grabbing a railing near the theater and keeps his hold by kicking as hard as he can an hysterical woman trying to grab him to save herself from being swept away. For West, there is little successful decency.

A bit improbably, West continues his metaphoric structure of the novel by showing the clinging and injured Tod fantasizing further work on his painting, "The Burning of Los Angeles." It is a refined extension of the scene he is in, with the mob heightened to torching the city and scapegoating the masqueraders. In the great bonfire of shoddy,

he was using the innumerable sketches he had made of the people who come to California to die; the cultists of all sorts, economic as well as religious, the wave, airplane, funeral and preview watchers—all those poor devils who can only be stirred by the promise of miracles and then only to violence. A super "Dr. Know-All Pierce-All" had made the necessary promise and they were marching behind his banner in a great united front of screwballs and screw boxes to purify the land. No longer bored, they sang and danced joyously in the red light of the flames.

With some novelistic illegitimacy, I suggest, West has slipped in some of his ideology of the threat of American demagogic politics, though no pierce-all messiah has been developed, and anyway might well not be appropriate to the Homeric catatonia of the apolitical locusts of America. The 1930s "progressive" again sticks through the perceptive artist.

Tod portrays himself in his painting as a masquerader pursued by the resentful mob, one who "picked up a small stone to throw before continuing his flight," perhaps not only the basic masquerader-mob relation (as with Adore and Homer) but an image of West's small defiant gesture in writing an artistic novel against mass America and its political threat. The art fantasy ends with Tod being pulled to safety by the police. He has "the presence of mind to give Claude's [prestigious] address" to be taken home to. Hearing the siren screaming in the police car, "at first he thought he was making the noise himself. He felt his lips with his hands. They were clamped tight. He knew then it was the siren. For some reason this made him laugh and he began to imitate the siren as loud as he could." Hysteria is all.

This screaming end to the novel caps several themes. As with "The Burning of Los Angeles," or all the males' obsessional attraction to the love-goddess masquerade of the autoerotic Faye, or the Hollywood fakery and role-playing, no one escapes the madness. Even self-conscious Tod (and West) might just as well, with whatever private ironies, scream along since none can truly exempt themselves from the American mob psychology. But is the artist (in and out of the fiction) just clowning here? West has insistently made the point, with Harry Greener (and earlier with Willie Shrike and Beagle Darwin), that clowning becomes a compulsive mechanism. And who is faking when fakery is all? And how does one tell the screamer from the siren, the self from the mob? In masquerading hysteria, Tod is hysterical. And in playing with artful hysteria, perhaps so is West.

The culminating sense of *The Day of the Locust* I take to be that curious Westean multiple-take, the mixture of obsessional clowning, bitter prophecy, self-conscious irony, and hysterical mergence. In a two-generation perspective, West's political prophecy of the ravaging American mob psyche seems overdone, an ideological twisting of the "morbid apathy" but endless adaptability of American mass consciousness. Perhaps that remains debatable. Besides, the pattern and tropes of the novel also suggest another view. The fiction starts out with a studio-lot counterfeit, which is compassionately extended to the whole city and its denizens, and even to nature. This carries through the various masquerades of the fiction, including more than one earlier "mock riot" which rehearses the final mob scene, which itself but provides rehearsal for the apocalyptic mob scene of "The Burning of Los Angeles," which after all is just a fantasy. The infinite regresses of modernist art, stylistically determining for West in spite of his not quite meshed political ideology, may also be the final shape of the meaning—and one faithful to the masquerading materials and the southern California ambience. For, contrary to some literal minded readers who miss the multiple-takes, the end is not exactly an apocalypse: there is no such implied cosmic order, only its grotesquely pathetic "screwball" and "screwbox" simulation. Clearly for Nathanael West, the world does not make sense, including that of the revelation of the end of time.

Even his embittered Hollywood mob has only parodied a revolutionary riot—just a momentary and unfocused bit of rending, stomping, sexual-sadistic play, madness, not the "civil war" West passingly dabbles with. The masqueraders show no more purpose: "automatons" not gratuitously smashed (Homer, Adore, Earl's testicles, the Mont St. Jean set), retain hardly any more authenticity than unfazable cork-Faye, or Tod's self-bemused hysteria, or the whole media and machine faked scene. The mob may erratically and pointlessly riot, the masqueraders may dance on in their role-playing marathon, but no one gets anywhere, not much really happens of lasting meaningfulness, though the very nothingness seems significant.

Granted that perhaps the final coherence of *The Day of the Locust* may not be altogether clear. (The metaphoric literalism about the end by many obviously obtuse critics should properly warn the sophisticated reader to examine it more closely.) I have suggested of various places in the novel some contradictions of tone, of formal organization, of muddled mob-masquerader dichotomizing around Homer, of the inadequate central consciousness of Tod, and of some ideological political impositions by West. *The Day of the Locust* stands as an intriguing and suggestive, and sometimes intense and insightful, but badly flawed novel. Of course, it is better than most fiction in the Hollywood subgenre (or at least of the half-hundred or so that I have read) and remains a worthwhile piece of American cultural exposé.

Yet in summary I want also to suggest that West does partly

achieve a brilliant ironic perspective. Remaining hard-eyed faithful to his Hollywood-American realities (and again I note the
basic "realism"), the author did not finally provide a "promised
end," only fractured masquerades of one. His evident paranoia
about America, and his prophetic sense of a doomed civilization,
was involuted. He thus recognizes that even in falsity and outrage and violence little escapes the mechanized passivity which
was the basic (and base) condition of sensibility for the developing technocracy. The ravaging of the urban land by the
petit bourgeois locusts, though expressing truly some of the anxieties of the individual and cultural malnutrition of America becoming Hollywood, was but another masquerade. The petit bourgeois, main resentful repository of the puritan heritage and related delusions (as the American lower middle class still is), only
appeared to be at war with the exploitative romanticism of the
dream factory. The result was rather more fusion than revolt.
The repressed American character was partly being transformed
by its fraudulent Hollywood dreams, a neither/nor inauthenticity
considerably expanded since West's time, until it now appears
that the mediaized locusts (the still resentful and nasty lower-
middle-class sensibility, slicked-up and manipulatively aggrandizing) dominates not only much of the culture but the politics.

    West's essentially ironic images of mock rioting, synthetic am-
bience, and costuming become flesh—the endlessly dancing cork,
the compulsive clowning, the rehearsal for debacle, the bemused
hysteria, the militant apathy, the endless grotesquery—prophesize
the total masquerade. With a mixture of compassion and fear,
he perceived the insatiable longing for some final violence, some
masquerade-ending negation. But he, too, was rather role-playing
the prophet as artist, though sardonic perceptivity undercut any
too-large claim. For the appropriate end to a life of masquerade,
and to a fraudulent civilization, is only a masquerade become all
reality. And that is the saddest as well as the truest apocalypse.

Chapter Five

Beyond Masquerading: Conclusions

The Pleasures of Pessimism

A first time reader of the fictions of Nathanael West, I have often found, will object to the harshness, the negativeness, the hopelessness, the pessimism.[1] So he or she will emphatically say. It strikes me as the most appropriate American response. Our popular culture, commentators generally acknowledge, has long displayed a fervent belief in a benign deity or a hopeful promise or a manifest destiny or an inevitable progress, and similar notions, around some insistent faith in almost any sort of up-and-on reaching. From a Westean view, we may see this as a crazy cultural landscape of hump-backed hills of "positive thinking," positive believing, positive anything, intersected by pollution-thick rivers of dishonesty and delusion. Pathetically, the inhabitants scurry around as grotesque little monsters claiming hopeful faiths, though a bit suspect in insisting on affirmative responses from everyone to their sick dreams. Still, they play at a touching geniality to testify that all will be for the best, somehow. At their nicest, they may admit that their hyped dreams are not quite true, but they can be made to work. As popular faith, the "best of all possible worlds" script might be traced back to the rise of an anxiously new and dominant middle class in eighteenth-century Western Europe. Secularized functional rationality, religious pieties displaced on to the market and the State, and contradictory mythologies of exalted individual gratification and willful applied power —in America, such ideologies could become a mania. America has long been the society where optimistic pronouncements appear to be incurable symptoms of disorder, or where positive slogans serve as national fetishes.

Our politics provides especially gross, though by no means exclusive, examples of "positive" anti-thought. Since the Great War (during which West grew into a somewhat cynical adolescence), they included smug appeals to "Saving the World for Democracy," a weirdly booming and ever better "Normalcy," and even the Great Depression "New Deal" (in which, said the president in a highly popular bit of camouflage, "we have nothing to fear but fear itself"), and an even more brutal total war in which we were bringing to the entire world the "Four Freedoms" of the good life. The retreaded optimistic lies since then (and West's violent end) included those for more wars, and other happily glossed proliferating destructions, decorated with such comical affirmations as a "New Frontier," then "The Great Society," and now (at the time of writing) yet another national campaign glossed with "a positive hope for America" and a "belief in America's great future" as "the shining city on a hill." The hill, of course, is of rubbish, and the shine may be that of putresence, if not of fatal radiation.

Our public manners have long demanded an energetic pseudo-geniality, including "boosterism" (West's youth), "super salesmanship" (for more than half a century), and strangling masks of "niceness." Much apparently serves as an essential part of what a shrewd social commentator has labeled our "civic religion." Not to partake of the optimism is not only disloyal but blasphemous.

Any brief survey of such poisonous positiveness should be sufficient justification for intellectual and artistic pessimism, like the Westean, as mandatory antidote. Still, the smiling toxicity is so pandemic one might reflect further. Perhaps much of the optimism in American public posturing can be seen as partly necessary, even imperative. At a practical level, commercial-consumer culture requires false faiths and spurious hopes in things and services and material symbols. The endless pursuit of our typical middle-class products and statuses must depend on magical, not rational and prudential, purposes; hence, the rhetorical religiosity around them. Once upon a time it was known as idolatry. Even many of the most ardent devotees of the happy American way decently pause now and again to admit that the superjets and electric carving knives, the advanced nuclear plants and peacocked videoboobery, and all the smogged statistics, salvational pills, anxious accumulations, and lavish distractions, do not provide all that much virtue and other gratification. What West, then, angrily labeled "the surfeit of shoddy" is no marginal or accidental characteristic of the system. Along with the endless processing of most natural and human qualities into a terrible and all-encompassing "waste," the crass surfeit is of the essence. It takes a drastically forced positiveness to even partly disguise the obvious fatuousness and futility of much of what we have, say, do, and feel.

An extremely positive view of the future as well as the immediate seems required to counter the awareness of anxious desperation in a counterfeit ordering. We may reasonably suspect that the whole process could not survive without its disguising. Dehumanizing "needs," argues Ivan Illich, must be fabricated and affirmed to hold the whole thing together for the advantage of some. The expansionism, the endless enlargement, becomes not only an economic necessity to avoid confrontation and collapse (as Robert Heilbroner, and other political economists, argue), but a psychological and ideological imperative. Only overcharged hopes, with optimism the lubricant, keep the American mechanism going. Stop to consider and it may screech and short out.

Whatever the other gratifications and exploitations, the "bourgeois order" as we know it depends on and demands an exceptionally optimistic faith, intensive in hope as well as in other capital. But cultures must be seen as dialectical, an endless counterpoint—such is the nature of the intellectual life. And this holds even when unwanted, or when, as in recent American intellectual history, the processors package and peddle, adapt and co-optate, most heterodoxy into the main stream. In contrast to popular public culture, much of American intellectual minority culture, from the Puritan casuists through the figures of our major literature

(Hawthorne and Melville, Faulkner and Eliot), has insisted on more negative and bleak views. No doubt some of this has been revulsive, scornfully defensive—and therefore sometimes over-done?—against the polluted river of bland and positive views. Self-definition in an amorphous and consuming culture must be (as, in other realms, our adolescents so often discover) by reaction, frequently defiant.

It may have been an ex-English writer in Hollywood, Aldous Huxley, who a generation ago first insisted that American artistic pessimism partook of the same giganticism and overdoing as other things American—our landscapes, buildings, industrialism, public hyperbole, and other wastings. But more than a century earlier, the French historian Alexis de Toqueville noted that cultivated culture in such alienating circumstances as the American scene might encourage the extreme and grotesque. Certainly West's fictions may be partly so characterized, and in context they must be understood as reactions to the prevailing popular temper, that is, as antioptimism.

On the whole, the optimism/pessimism division in America functions not just as a temperamental or moral cast of sensibility but also as an expression of cultural class-identity: public-popular culture generally affirmative, intellectual-minority culture more nullifidian. Granted, the cultural-class divisions can show odd permutations and striking reversals. Some noted American writers— Mark Twain and Hart Crane come to mind—went from exalted affirmations of American myths into final despairing rejections. We also have traditions of poetic visionaries, such as that running from Whitman through Ginsberg and beyond, which expand the optimism into ecstatic mystical questings—not at all what the stock pietists of the American positive want and mean. (Besides, there usually appears a harshly critical side to our prophets of embracement, dark views of the body politic as well as national soul.)

Modern America has also always had at least its share of trimmer-intellectuals, cultivated institutional apologists and easily prostituted mandarins and writers, who, like the sardonic Nathanael

West turning out standard Hollywood script pap, have "sold out." (So such betrayal of the critical used to more candidly be called; when, of course, almost everything gets denatured, exploited, processed, hustled, celebritized, corrupted, it may be difficult to even relatively keep up such moral discriminations.) We have also repeatedly seen in America variations of majoritarian pietism, intellectuals mawkishly identifying against their own identity and function. So with the "progressive" and "Popular Front" cultural politics of the 1930s, which West curiously, perhaps bravely, given his politics, friends, and times, seems to have rejected. Playing "progressive" often led to an optimistically sentimental glorification of the "common man." Something basically similar reappeared in the "anti-elitist" intellectualism of the 1960s, and is still around. Its mannerisms include out-proletarianizing the lower classes in dress, speech, and murky notions. A recent image of it, which could provide grotesque material for a neo-Westean fiction, might be of a denim-grad academic (or other ideological hustler) splattering clichés plagarized from "minorities" and "Third World" fanaticism, while denouncing intellectual and artistic (indeed, any thoughtful) discrimination as "arrogantly elitist." Its masquerade usually includes displacing a sense of justice with sentimentality for victims and a patronizing benevolence. It also likes to posture as hopeful, oh-so-democratic and ever-optimistic. So goes some of our intellectual inverted snobbery.

Still, the negative/positive division in American culture between popular and intellectual responses has long been around and probably retains some essential truth. Disinterestedly put, openness to pessimism in American life seems to be a crucial quality of sensibility for, if not "high seriousness," at least some degree of cultural sophistication. That persons of intellectual disposition and role may sometimes sentimentally and opportunistically play at other identities, become pietists of popular optimisms, no more disposes of the general point than does an awareness that we also fortunately can find dissident and heterodox heritages of American folkish criticism and iconoclasm. Certainly it might be possible to find some authentic yet optimistic American intellectuals and artists, though I know none, can name none, and would probably doubt their continuing reality. At least for elaborate historical reasons, pessimism is where the larger intelligence is mostly at.

I do not mean to suggest that some intellectual criticism (excluding, of course, that large part of the "secondary" writings which are academic or commercial hackwork) has not raised concern about West's emphatic negativism, as in discussing his "extreme art," his obsessional "disease," and his "nihilism." But since such commentators also show awareness that West's art does not shape out as the most pessimistic in modernism—it is really rather mild compared with Franz Kafka's or Samuel Beckett's—the charge usually comes with considerable qualifications. We also need not argue with such rhetoric since one reader's nihilistic illness may be, with a slight change of emphasis, another reader's tough-minded wisdom. West himself sometimes bemusedly annotated his pessimism. In the middle of *The Day of the Locust* artist Tod notes to himself his pleasure in his "Jeremiah" role, the "strong feeling of satisfaction" his "dire conclusion" about the violent future of the country gives him. He asks, but does not directly answer, the question: "Were all prophets of doom and destruction such happy men?"

Frequently, yes. Compulsive optimists, like those who make up the middle-American mob with "positive" thinking and "Have a nice day" pseudo-feeling, may well turn bitter, perhaps viciously resentful like West's "locusts," when finally recognizing the negative. On the other hand, those with more negative expectations, like Nathanael West and his artist, may get its special pleasures, from the smug "I warned you" to the exalting *amor fati* of the cosmic fatalist. To embrace harsh destiny, as Nietzsche argued, may be to achieve one of the higher styles of gratification. Given what mostly seem to be the ways of the world, and human mortality, a very good case can be made for negative expectations, and the pleasures of appropriate fulfillment. Who can reasonably doubt that pessimists, on the whole, have the odds on their side? Furthermore, if the primary duty of the intellectual is to try not to be deluded (and West, in his serious art, was certainly an intellectual), then he, above all, should recognize the negative case. (Indeed, an unpessimistic intellectual should be a suspect figure, either as to his competence or his intentions.) A pessimistic view, of course, should not be equated with the grumpy, the dour, the unresponsive, the life-denying—in sum, the unhappy. A negativism unto nihilism often produces "gaiety" (Nietzsche, again). But the positive results of the negative may even go beyond that joy in defiant acceptance, which includes the elimination of lesser anxieties. "Survival," notes Terence De Pres in studying those who outlasted the Nazi death camps, "required not having hope." (I take this to mean reasonable hope, not delusion, which is always around.)

To parody the Saul who masqueraded himself as St. Paul, hope and faith, though apparently not charity, characterize foolishness and fanaticism rather more than intelligence and a sense of the actual. They provide motives for illusion and delusion, and thus for disillusion and breakdown. Sanity, and its modicum of pleasure, lie elsewhere. Pessimists, in sum, are good candidates for happiness as well as truth.

The Shapes of Denial

Since the negative tonalities and pessimisms seem to take such a large place in reader responses to West's fictions, we might glance again at some of his central negations. *The Dream Life of Balso Snell* denied optimistic faiths in culture, dramatized as arty role-playing. (The mockery of religion there remained incidental, though importantly establishing the tone of blasphemy and looking forward to the later writings.) However skittishly fanciful in literary costuming, the method was the classical satirist's one of undercutting in which basic body motives—the excremental and the sexual—directed, and betrayed, the pretensions to truth and other virtues. Such unmasking of cultural claims sensibly exposed art as an improper realm for faith and hope. The literary life came out as mostly fakery; culture does not provide adequate human answers.

That pessimistic mockery of arty poses, however, did show some amusement and exuberance—illustrating some of the happy pleasures of denial? The frequent straining, raggedness, overdoing, which mars the early novella may be attributed to a forcing because the immature author retains some optimistic hopes and romantic-fantasy faith in playing the modernist artist. As West's own metaphors have it, this is cultural masturbation, thus perhaps the excess of verbal manipulation. But he was sufficiently serious not to be merely earnest about his tough-wise perception of the inadequacy of culture and its masquerades.

Miss Lonelyhearts, however, does something yet more serious than the quasi-confessional burlesque of the artist. It goes after the more profound cultural role-playing which is religion. As my detailed explication tried to emphasize, West attacked Christianity at the core—the sick-saint and the question of suffering—not at the issues usually taken up by the more genial skeptic, such as "institutional corruption," historical excrescences, and the needs for social reforms. The ultimate answers provide ultimate counterfeits. Faith is the failure, trying to live by religious hope a fatal delusion. Little if any good comes from it, and the religious masquerades of reality turn out to be demands for destruction.

It might be countered that West, too, shows an ultimate vision of reality, a metaphysical belief in disorder, entropy, and the incommensurability of the human and the world. Perhaps he underwent a revelation, reverse style, in which he believed the voices out of the human whirlwind of anxious chaos. Fair enough; *Miss Lonelyhearts*, then, carries nothing less than a religious vision, though one directed at denial, the downward way to wisdom.

It may be that atheism has been given as bad a name by its bland rationalist partisans as Christianity has by its sweetish pietists. The authentic case for both, as Kierkegaard and Nietzsche remind us, may be rather more drastic and demanding than often put. As the Westean atheist insists, no religious or anti-religious view holds up very well which fails to recognize that in reality *everyone* suffers, and many suffer far beyond, and quite outside, the justifications proffered by religious doctrine or by functional rationality. And most faiths, West insisted, display as essential to them the masquerades, the role-playing, which confirm their in-authenticity. Possibly, in other times and places, there could be simple full religious faith, but much of it is necessarily unlikely in twentieth-century America, and even less likely with anyone who could plausibly read *Miss Lonelyhearts* (or my discussion of it).

In his atheist parable, West also extends his mockeries to other costumings than the traditionally religious: not only the "escapes" to hedonism, the simple life, art, primitivism, and romance (as adumbrated by the Shrikes) but more broadly to the media-debased popular culture "dreams." Such great "betrayal" of the actual and integral self reinforces, I suggest, the case against the more grandiloquent "Christ dream." Grand or shoddy, all of them are hysterical costumings. Yet in reexamining West's iconoclasms, one should recognize that he almost always places them in compassionate contexts (perhaps furthered by the especially strong Jewish sense of suffering). And the Westean perspective remains pertinent. The surfeit of shoddy dreams, religious and other, continues two generations later, as does the need for a fuller compassion.

The following *A Cool Million* may be so much less than *Miss Lonelyhearts* partly because the compassion seems hard to find around the Horatio Alger dolt, the fascist-nativist demagogue, and the other caricature scoundrels and fools. West, perhaps imitating the merely clever Perelman, tried to be glibly funny but came out contemptuously angry. By the failure of his depression burlesque-satire, curiously, we may see that persuasive and true negation paradoxically requires some degree of sympathetic entry into, even identification with, that which is to be denied.

To fully perceive the bad, which is what pessimism is about, means to see into, under, and through what is—more especially that which appears good and hopeful, at least to the optimists. But we, West included, may temperamentally lack entry into and under, and therefore may not be able to really see through, a fascist demagogue, which negates much of *A Cool Million*. The crass handling of the Lemuel-innocent in that fiction poses a var-

iant difficulty. My analysis suggested signs of West's own historical
and political naiveté. But he insisted on disguising his own innocence in a superior, and often sniggering, comic pose. The anti-
masquerader was smothered in his own masquerade.

Surely his iconoclastic talents were defeated in *A Cool Million*.
He angrily rejected, considerably for external political reasons before very fully perceiving, the powers of the American success
myth. That makes our national faith in ignorant aggrandizement
merely silly instead of the larger evil it should probably be seen
as. American optimism about "success" would seem to be a far
more insidious process than West allows. He quite lacked the
empathetic irony of his literary peer in Hollywood (Fitzgerald) that
in America "nothing fails like success." Perhaps one could suggest,
then, that in his third book as well as in some of his life, West's
failure was his concern with American-style "success." He sadly
illustrates some of the costs of that naive masquerade of a fuller
humanness.

The Day of the Locust may partly improve upon the previous
book not only because of the evident compassion for the Hollywood margins (where West felt himself to be for a time, though
the shallow stock Yalie narrator points up an ambivalence which
weakens the work) but also because of the more direct concern
for failure and defeat. Where the political prophecy of *A Cool
Million*, the takeover of populist fascism, though understandable
in terms of the American depression, stands as too naive and
literal, the mock-rioting of the petit bourgeois locusts in the last
fiction merits (as I argued in some detail) a partly more subtle
and lasting interpretation. While both draw on essentially the
same grim sense of the American social character, the irony of
the endless masquerade points beyond any merely callow political
doom-saying. That would be too Americanly innocent, a pessimism the mere reverse of the stock American optimism, not just
because history should be viewed as more dialectical than that
allows but because the real world is real, and masquerading it has
to come a cropper.

The imperative realities of bodily motives in *The Dream Life* of *Balso Snell*, the realities of discord and suffering in *Miss Lonely-hearts*, the realities of the Great Depression in *A Cool Million*, become in *The Day of the Locust* the unnamed and not directly dramatized but nonetheless insistent reality of selfhood, however disguised and distorted. West, unlike some of those who have imitated parts of his manner, was no epiphenomenalist, no mere phantasmagorist. He held hard to basic realisms of the body, the society, and the person. Thus the anger and the horror at the poses, the religious dreams, the social myths, the Hollywood masquerading, remain. While the fictions may be viewed as tools of the reality demanding pessimism, we should also recognize that disciplined denial is far more than mere anger, denouncement, or any just righteous rejection. A true pessimism finally reveals a deeper affirmation of the human.

Dark Laughter

All this emphasis on the negative way to wisdom should not be allowed to obscure the humor. Memoirs suggest that West was frequently a genial and even funny fellow amid what one of his friends described as his "incurable pessimism." His fictions may cling to memory most strongly with bits of the bemused grotesquery: in *The Dream Life of Balso Snell*, the poet in the anus of the Trojan Horse, and the arty audience covered with excrement—the reversals that a long overdigested culture have brought us to; in *Miss Lonelyhearts*, Faye Doyle's maritime disrobing, and the search for the jewel in teaser Mary Shrike's cleavage (a medal for the hundred yard dash)—some twists of puritanized sexuality in its decadence; in *A Cool Million* the whorehouse Americana—a pattern of childishly fancied-up grossness for our synthetic consumer culture; in *The Day of the Locust*, the macho dwarf, the studio "dream dump" of cast-off props of histories, gods, and other romances, and the incongruous details of California Southland decoration—all guileless self-parodies. But there are many amusing images. West's fictions display a comic sense ranging from bemusement to hilarity.

Much of our laughter, of course, is not light but the darker cast we have learned to recognize from surrealism (and its popular American adaption in the "black humor" of the 1960s—the tag *"humeur noir"* had been spread by surrealist polemicist André Breton some years earlier). More broadly, such incongruities draw upon the anguished (and usually not directly humorous) awareness of disparities in the existentialist tradition of western European culture in the past century and a half. Thus the risible incongruities less depend on deviation from a sensible norm (more or less the standard for classical and neoclassical satiric humor) than on the disparities and grotesqueries in an absurd universe. The excremental or sexual takes over, especially, as West has it, when one pretends to high culture or religion. Some metaphors, as with Christianity's "rock of faith" and "conversion," become fatal mad metaphysics. The merely decorative, be it a religious icon, a Hollywood image of romance, or a silly American tale of success, turns into a devouring mechanism. Some of West's comic techniques certainly fit Henri Bergson's argument in *Laughter* that comedy shows the mechanical overtaking the human. But more generally, disproportion seems central: a trope turns into a monstrous conceit which replaces all mere reality; a joke twists into a pained infinite regress of laughing at the "laugh at the laugh"; a cleverly defensive pose (as with Beagle Darwin or Harry Greener) takes off on its own, its human author becoming the automaton of his masquerade. A wry little effort at a petty bit of ordering (Lonelyhearts, Homer Simpson) slides into a maniacal compulsion. A romantic yearning (a Hollywood dream or other debased fantasy) swells into an obsessional disease which sickens all mere human reality.

Much of West's jokiness plays with a lesser "sick humor" (as it was later to be called—"Besides that, how did you enjoy the play, Mrs. Lincoln?"). This mostly depends on the violation of taboos. Thus the anti-Semitic wisecracks by the Jewish author (in every work), the crudely ethnic buffoonery (*A Cool Million* especially, but also in the other writings), the comic descriptions of a cripple (Peter Doyle in *Miss Lonelyhearts*), a dwarf (Abe

Kusich in *The Day of the Locust*), a hunchback and potential suicide (Janey Davenport in *The Dream Life of Balso Snell*), a dying man (Harry Greener in the last novel), and pathetic neurotics (almost everyone and everywhere). No doubt such "disgusting honesty" of the comic artist releases the repressed, and quite probably depends on his own inadequate superego. In recognizing the service to our psychic awareness, we need not admire as a person the comic artist—a grossly sentimental confusion often applied to performers (for example, Chaplin) as well as writers.

But some of the Westean comic strategies take more profound directions, deploying the great ancient arts of blasphemy. Patently, all faiths necessarily depend on falsification, and all worships come out perverse. The blasphemer correctly reverses the process. To reveal a saint as a pious flea or the imitation of Christ as a descent into psychotic catatonia carries more powerful shocks of repressed recognition than stock "sick humor." To see brave American patriots as pathetic clods or fascist demagogues provides salutary information. To recognize artistic devotees of the imagination as masturbatory adolescents (of all ages) or doltish little voyeurs helps in a necessary cultural sophistication. It is more than amusing realism to perceive the poet as con man (Snodgrasse), the love goddess as indifferent whore (Faye), and most of the righteous as nasty little sadists. The blasphemer merely strips the costuming, denies the masquerade.

West, of course, did not "invent" blasphemous humor, though he applied the ancient deflationary arts to some particularly pertinent American pieties. The fusion of laughter and bitterness, comedy and pessimism, reveal old European lineages; recall not only Rochester and Swift (the final book of *Gulliver's Travels*) and Voltaire but much wider literary reaches into the sardonically grotesque all the way back two and a half millenia to Euripides. Indeed, West as a college student published an essay on that most blasphemous of the Greek dramatists in a campus magazine; while it was brief and sophomoric, it did suggest the writer to come: Euripides (and West) is "a religious man" and "a charlatan," a "satirist" and "a man of feeling."[2]

Other lines of Westean diabolic amusement have been traced to more immediate literary places by several scholars, to probable "sources" in Baudelaire, Rimbaud, Huysmans, and Anatole France. Favorite painters of West's, previously noted, such as Magnasco, Goya, and Max Ernst, may be added to the lineage of the grotesque. No doubt the points noted here could be much elaborated, the lines extended to further encompass other blasphemous mockeries, the savage indignation of the harsher satirists, additional surrealists and their forerunners, and the broader flow of existential doubt and absurdity. But the pedantic games of "sources" is less the issue here than the awareness of the approximate lineaments of a relevant direction to what West was doing. Half a century ago he was domesticating European traditions of dark laughter in the American scene.

I believe that deserves emphasis. American literary humor, with but few curious exceptions, has until recent times been all too American. That means that much of it has been gross, as with the frontier braggart ("the man from Pike County, Missouri" burlesqued in *A Cool Million*), or compulsively and simple-mindedly exploitative vaudeville (Harry Greener, or Bob Hope), or even more disgustingly bland (Washington Irving, the Tom Sawyerish Twain, popular magazine humor for some generations, the larger part of commercial movie and television comedy). True, there are some other bits, and it might be possible to link in spirit West's fictions with other sardonic American pessimists, such as, say, the absurdist Melville of "Bartleby, the Scrivener," or the disillusioned final Mark Twain, or the cynical Ambrose Bierce. Still, most American humor, literary as well as popular, has been crude, genial, optimistically crass. West, except in mockery of it, went elsewhere.

Part of West's impetus, as I see it, was the Americanization of certain mordant aspects of European modernism. While, for example, "The Chamber of Horrors, Inanimate and Animate Hideosities," is pure Americana, as are the "lovelorn" dilemmas and the Hollywood masquerades, the contemptuous distance is quite un-American. The bemused disgust, the twisted smile at the outrageous, the barking laugh at the utterly repulsive, probably depend on a sense of immediate confrontation yet psychic removal. Perhaps a sense of Jewish marginality, the incompletely assimilated outsider, contributed to it, but so certainly did an ingrained reference to more alien images and standards of denial. Certainly in his time the Westean fusion of American materials and a cultivated European modernism seems a curious balancing act. The expatriate modernist Americans did not have much of it, in their more complete rejections, and the returned cultural exiles (Malcolm Cowley, et al) often rejected their rejections and over-embraced the American scene.

West, incompletely excoriating his own romanticism which he also saw in his American materials, had a certain compassion in his savaging. The more completely foreign observers do not. Reading truly distant European accounts of American culture, from de Tocqueville and Mrs. Trollope through Lawrence and Sartre and beyond, one may sense that the responder has to be inside the American fantasies while yet beyond them to properly recognize their monstrosity. Somehow West, the half-masqueraded American, was both inside and outside those fantasies, painfully laughing at himself.

Probably blasphemous humor such as West's, whether it be in laughing darkly at American myths of religion, success, culture, or romance, requires some vestigial belief—or it would lack the sacrilegious energy. As Plato insisted, a major impetus to comic poetry is impiety to the gods and the State. But as the authoritarian philosophers (and what systematic—"essentialist"—thinker is not authoritarian?) did not make quite clear, most literary art plays with words and contradictory realities and is therefore open to comic possibilities. West, it may be granted, represents a conscious extreme of the blasphemous, an outraging comic perspective. Once properly immersed in the Westean, one may be inclined to read, say, portraits of the artist as masturbatory exercises, religious visions as pathetic psychoses, American success stories as nasty frauds, and romantic masquerades as portents of doom. That, anyway, would probably be the ultimate service of such art. Plato, then, if you believe in the pieties of order, was certainly right to expel the poets: they may make us darkly laugh. West certainly can.

Nathanael West in American Literary History

Compared with some of his significant contemporaries, West's fictions hardly reach full-scale grotesquery, such as the rather awful hatreds of Louis-Ferdinand Céline, or, to take one of the few American prose writers of West's time with a surrealist sensibility, the fractured buffoonery of Henry Miller. But these three extreme comedians turned out to be more relevant a generation later than the earnest naturalists, such as Dreiser, Dos Passos, Farrell et al., or such sentimental-realists as Lewis and Steinbeck. Fitzgerald and Hemingway and Faulkner may have had less pertinence to the American imaginative prose of the past couple of decades than West. And so on, down the historical list. Separated from the ponderous historians, history is often a weird thing, not least the literary side of it.

It would not only be foolish but a blindness to the history of histories to find a definitive place for Nathanael West in American literary history. In the first couple of decades following his last book, he hardly appears in any of the literary chronologies, catalogs, or expositions. In the next couple of decades he appears more and more frequently. While for reasons of both the limits of the work—quite literally—and the peculiarity of the view, it seems unlikely that West will be accounted, anthologized, exploited academically or commercially, and the rest, as "a major American author," he probably for some time to come will have a signicant place in the literary record.

One can note several ironies around that. For one evident thing, West's literary ambitions—writing a burlesque, an antireligious fable, a slapdash satire, a Hollywood exposé—were never large in scope. His reach, except for a certain kind of intense insight, was small, marginal. Any expansion of his literary role tends to obscure that simple truth. The considerable enlargement of his reputation in the recent past, in spite of the obviously truncated literary life, may also obscure the likelihood that it has little expansive possibilities. I do not know how to factually demonstrate it but I have a sense that West's reputation may have peaked some time back (in the early 1970s?). However, much of literary history, like other histories, serves institutional motives (and commercial, pedagogical, and other "professional" practices). Official reputation relates only dimly to aesthetic and intellectual qualities, and to the experience of authentic readers. Fashionableness, not least that of West, may be an intriguing subject, but it rarely can be an honest or adequate concern.

Part of what raised West in fashionableness was a broader change in the literary and moral *zeitgeist* in America (or more properly, in certain intellectual circles). While literary, and other, reputations certainly in part come about as the result of accidents, chance, gratuitous developments, they also appear to partly reflect certain climates of ideas and feelings. A generation ago there spread a disenchantment with the blandly conformist ideology that we now look upon as characterizing the 1950s, and which wildly but woozily spread in the half-dozen years of the American-Vietnam War after the middle of the 1960s. A response to existentialist ideas and literature partly prepared it. Minority social and political iconoclasms were certainly central to it. A greater variety of *recognized* behaviors and styles contributed to a more varied consciousness and, since the relation of cultural and social consciousness usually seems to be partly circular, a greater variety of artistic expression contributed to social variation. Modernism in the arts, the now dominant appearing movement in Western culture from about the mid-nineteenth to the mid-twentieth centuries, came to a major backwash just about the time it had most fully inundated the academy, and thus wetted the greatest number of readers. Aesthetically, the odd and bizarre were increasingly in fashion. Exaggerated styles, whether in painting, costuming, religiousity, or prose, were more acceptable. Many moral as well as aesthetic decorums seemed fractured, as the Westean sensibility required.

Other conditions and symptoms of the atmosphere of the times could be noted, such as a revival of things from the 1930s—partly nostalgia industries, partly enlarged leftist political concerns, partly cyclic academic manufacturings. This goes with a pathetic compulsion in American culture, and its huckstering, given the obvious self-awareness of its amorphousness and thinness, to keep churning up more bits and strands of a "usable past." (To my eye, it has become a synthetic frenzy, and one which we literary critics and cultural historians have helped give more than its due.) That West, unlike so many of the naturalistic writers of the 1930s, combined social-cultural anger with an artful style, probably has considerable relevance to his revival in a more sophistication-demanding time (some could call it decadence). West's obsessive concern with "mass culture," i.e., the mythicized responses involved with, and exploited by, popular public media, may have seemed especially appropriate in the later period when the mass-media, far more pervasive and dominant, became the "primary curriculum" (Postman) of American learning and sensibility.

But my purpose here is less to limn a thumbnail cultural history than merely to suggest that an ambience appropriate to a more widespread and intense interest in the fiction of Nathanael West had developed. Probably that is more important to his present recognition as a "significant minor novelist" than a more judicious acknowledgment of his exceptional artistry and insight. But perhaps there can be several ways of reading the history of a reputation, from West's very limited recognition in his lifetime (by interesting critics, mostly his friends, such as Fitzgerald, Edmund Wilson, Robert Coates), to an intense but quite limited audience and admiration (mid-1940s to mid 1950s), through the publication of his collected novels (1957) and then a great flurry of attention by well-known literary figures, unto the first biographical volume (1961), a number of competent studies (in the 1960s by Hyman, Comerchero, Reid, et al), a ponderous full-scale biography (1970), a number of academic anthologies of criticism (1970, 1971, 1973), proliferating studies (bibliographical, exegetical, comparative), and to apparently a fairly wide readership and standard recognition. History is what history does, or sometimes thinks it has done, and not least by those who enshrine pieces and pops of it.

"Influences," the ostensible relations of a writer to others, provides another simulation of literary history. On a backward perspective, this is the curious academic game called "sources" in which one claims "influences," "echoes," "parallels," and some rather more obscure relationships, between two texts, one usually earlier than that of the subject's. This has been done for West in detail—one cannot say "exhaustively" since it can never be definitive, nor often even highly persuasive, for there are not only sources for the sources but under the pedantic manners lies an endless ingenuity, a speculative exercise, in possible similarities and origins. Traditionally, it is rather narrowly done, as if most books were birthed from other, standardly recognized, books. More recently, some bookish hunters have pursued what are thought of as less meritorious sources—in West's case, a few comments on his possible use of comic strips and bad movies. I think it likely, though I have not pursued it, that there were many *negative* influences on West, including his acknowledged distaste for long naturalistic fictions, his evident parody of newspapers (I suspect him of having been a compulsive reader of them), and of other popular materials. But we all do sources selectively; while I have briefly noted a few likely ones, my perhaps biased emphasis has been on the European modernist parallels because that seems the most useful context for understanding West and his antagonist relation to his American culture.

"Influences" also go the other way, forward in time, to how a writer might effect later writers, which is certainly part of his works' history. The trouble here, of course, arises in that for a writer whose influence is relatively recent one's information must be more accidental than systematic. Still, a few obvious influences of West can be noted, especially since other writing sensibilities around the 1960s went into somewhat related orbits. Specific acknowledgments of some influence have been made by a number of writers of the American grotesque, from the deeply religious Flannery O'Connor to the cleverly bizarre John Hawkes. Some Holly-

wood novels, logically enough, show apparent influences from
The Day of the Locust, perhaps a bit in Alison Lurie's *Nowhere
City*, some laterally in David Madden's *Bijou*, certainly quite a bit
in Wright Morris's bemused concern with denaturing role-playing
in *Love Among the Cannibals*. But since West has long been recognized as providing an outstanding pass through the hump-
backed cultural hills of Hollywood, and somewhat more generally
of Southland decor, his influence might be detected in many writings utilizing that subject matter. (I have painfully detected some
Westean gestures in several different but equally obtuse and smug
recent sketches of such scenes.)

West's influence on "black humor" writings of the 1960s seems
likely, as with Kurt Vonnegut, Terry Southern, Donald Bar-
thelme, and others. Yet, of course, they could also have been colored
and toned by some of the same sources (surrealist, satiric, grotesque) that West was, as well as quite different ones, once we
recognize that a sense of the sardonically absurd responses to the
modern world have not been all that rare. Along with some other
critics, I strongly suspect that West influenced Joseph Heller
(*Catch 22*, but not much the other two novels), though I am not
sure how one would demonstrate it other than by broad similarities
of humor, grotesquery, iconoclasm, and nihilism. Some literary
historians have loosely suggested that West, one of the first identifiable Jewish-American writers on non-Jewish subjects, probably
had considerable effect on what has become the subgenre of Jewish-
American fiction. Possibly so, though one wonders uncomfortably
about what has become a dubious overconcern with cultural eth-
nicity. Certainly in the past generation West has become a marker
for sardonic awareness about aspects of American culture. Not surprisingly, those playing the prophet cite him, such as Paul Goodman (resentfully) and Norman Mailer (imitatively). But enough.
It would be no disservice to either literary history or to a larger
sense of American culture in the middle decades of the twentieth
century to cite Nathanael West as one of *the* authors to read.[3]

One way and another, the imaginative sensibility of Nathanael
West became, in spite of its peculiarity and extremity, relatively

mainstream in American literature, and beyond. (One can hardly claim more than that since American culture may be essentially without a center, and without very substantial coherence.) Perhaps it was the humor within pessimism and the odd mixture of compassionate grotesquery and bemusedly hard-eyed realism which did it. Perhaps, too, with proper historical irony, we may see much of this as another of the topsy-turvy delights of relentless negation.

Beyond the Masquerade?

The more interesting critics have emphasized that Nathanael West, in spite of the small volume and shape of his fiction, reveals an encompassing vision of debasing American "dreams," of the totality of cultural "decadence," even of the "decline of the West" and the apocalyptic end of a whole civilization. Certainly his heightened specifics do show not only a strong case for modern atheistic pessimism but a large informing spirit. For those at least partly willing to entertain such a *Weltanschauung*, West may be viewed as something more than a "minor" novelist of the American 1930s. Whatever its peculiarity or form, a thorough and profound perception of reality is never minor.

While I am inclined to entertain this view, yet I remain somewhat doubtful about major/minor and other boxes of literary history and academic propriety and aesthetic-moral hierarchy. For the critically responsive reader, too much attention to such concerns may defeat a more dialectical awareness, obscure the direct sensing of ambivalence, mixed effects, reversing ironies, and, especially, an awareness of the consuming nature of all masquerades, which I take to be the crucial Westean issue. While West may sensibly be viewed as a visionary of pessimism, he should also be seen as problematic (as I have tried in some detail to indicate), as the not quite resolvable ironist of masquerading.

One intriguing perplexity with the essential cast of West's sensibility might be recognized at its pessimistic center. Surely he is negative unto nihilism about usual optimisms—the universe never quite makes human sense. Yet what has not been much considered is the positive thrust which goes with this negativity. The intensity of the style, at its best, the powerful impetus to artistic shaping, as with *Miss Lonelyhearts* and parts of the other fictions, the moral fervor, when not reduced to Great Depression "progressive" ideology, and the will to an exposing truthfulness— these carry an emphatically affirmative sense of the mind and the self. West's very insistence on falsity and role-absurdity (there are no really evil characters in his fiction, no coherent badness) must presuppose other human possibility. The devastating exposure of masquerading, to use a not inappropriate existential language, requires a will to authenticity and fuller being.

It is not merely odd or grotesque to be an "automaton" (one of West's favorite tropes, direct or implicit)—a dismantled machine (Lemuel), a compulsive mechanism (Beagle and Harry), a masturbatory fantasy robot (Balso and Tod), a catatonic "coil" (Homer), a joke machine (Shrike), an impervious decorated cork (Faye), an hysterical circuit in a world of dead doorknobs (Lonely-hearts)—it is more, it is destructively untrue to both reality and the self. Thus somehow life might, and essentially must be, different. While there are no more good characters in West than evil ones, around most of his grotesques hangs a penumbra, a larger sense of mind, of will, of responsiveness, of compassion, of genuineness.

We know it by its insisted-upon absence. For in the Westean world the masquerades do not really work. The automatons go haywire. The endless role-players end as the most ugly and hopeless of cases. The dreams whoosh to destruction. West's insistence upon ineffectuality in his protagonists (and in much of his life, too) shows tones of endless frustration. The sense of ever-impending violence, the longing to break out, break through, or just ragingly break, confirms it. Without pushing my point to mere cleverness, I want to suggest strongly that the responsive reader detects something more than sardonic pessimism, soured romanticism, waste land symbology, mobs and masqueraders. After all, one strips masquerades to find. . . .

The very energy of West's disillusion, it might be said, posits the American utopian, the very intensity of the sardonic art demands a different and better life. West, I suggested, was the ancient mocking prophet, but he was also the energetically modern yearning American. The endlessly masquerading, and masquerade-breaking, author certainly disguises his positive yearnings. But they warp out in the life, not only in the naive "progressive" politics (otherwise unexplainable) and in the simultaneously self-hiding and self-exposing foolish role-playing (Ivy League dandy, Nimrod, Hollywood hack), but in the very hyperbole fused with realism in his fictions. Perhaps modernist West was finally authenticating the very old role of the cynical idealist, in and out of his fiction. Just as he was showing us about everyone else, his masquerading did not quite work. One of the most pessimistic of American writers insists, with whatever forlorn ironies, upon the positive, including that of going beyond all masquerades.[4]

Notes and References

Chapter One

1. For a compendium of the sociological, see *Role Theory: Concepts and Research,* ed. Bruce J. Biddle and Edwin J. Thomas (New York: Wiley, 1966), or the writings of Erving Goffman et al. While the notions go back to West's time, I do not suggest any direct relation between this jargonized obtuseness and West's masquerading. The widespread contemporary social-psychological notions of role-playing tend not only to hide the ancient origins, largely religious I think, of masks, personae, mythic identifications, and the like, but treat them as just affirmative requirements of social interaction, the therapeutic, etc., without recognizing them as a major modern disease.

2. Though I have examined other sources, I have confined most of my information here to the two standard academic biographies: James F. Light, *Nanthanael West, An Interpretative Study* (Evanston, 1971); and Jay Martin, *Nathanael West, The Art of His Life* (New York, 1970). Neither are responsible for my sometimes quite different interpretations of their material.

3. There are a number of studies commenting on, and perhaps sometimes exaggerating, West's role as a Jewish-American novelist. See, for example, Leslie A. Fiedler, "The Breakthrough: The American Jewish Novelist and the Fictional Image of the Jew," in *Recent American Fiction,* ed. Joseph J. Waldheimer (Boston, 1963), pp. 84–109. Miles Donald loosely argues that West's self-doubting irony was especially Jewish in *The American Novel and the Twentieth Century* (New York, 1978), pp. 162–66. Anxiety, and a certain kind of social paranoia, might have made a better case. For placement within the context of later Jewish fictionists, see Max F. Schulz, "Nathanael West's Desperate Detachment," in *Radical Sophistication, Studies in Contemporary Jewish American Novelists* (Athens, Ohio, 1969), pp. 36–55. There are related studies but I am most indebted to Eleanor Rackow Widmer and Sam Hardin for knowledgeable and intense discussion of the issues, though not for my conclusions. In confirmation

of several of my points here, I will note the anti-Semitism in each novel, and some less self-hating characteristics which might be related to the Jewish heritage.

4. For a synopsis of West's unpublished play, see *The Best Plays of 1938–39*, ed. Burns Mantle (New York: Dodd, Mead, 1939), pp. 427–28; and Martin, pp. 289 ff. For the film scripts, see also Martin, pp. 401–6. For other description of West's Hollywood work, see Tom Dardis, "Nathanael West: The Scavenger of the Back Lots," in *Some Time in the Sun: The Hollywood Years of Fitzgerald, Faulkner, Nathanael West, Aldous Huxley and James Agee* (New York, 1976), pp. 151–81. Dardis points out that West's *weekly* pay scale ranged from $200 to $450, though a long part of it was at $350 (p. 168). Two hundred a *month* was a comfortable, and above average, family living at that time. West's partnered story "treatments" in his later Hollywood days sold for from ten to twenty-five thousand dollars (p. 180), even when split and minus possible fees, a real fortune. But Dardis's literary comments seem rather silly, such as that West created a "myth" of Hollywood as a place of "sinister decay" (p. 181). My remarks on West's film work are based on the summaries provided by others and my viewing three films he helped script (*Five Came Back, The Spirit of Culver*, and *I Stole a Million*) which, reportedly, were not his worst. For a good discussion of the *Miss Lonelyhearts* movie mentioned below, see Dwight McDonald, "No Art and No Box Office," *Encounter* 13 (July 1959): 51–55.

5. See the rather cute sketches of Ruth McKenney, *My Sister Eileen* (New York: Random House, 1938) and *All About Eileen* (New York: Random House, 1952). But these do not tell us much about Eileen's or Ruth's fellow-traveling politics, which may have been influential on West.

6. So Martin reports, though he seems naive on the politics. Larry Ceplair and Steven England, *The Inquisition in Hollywood, Politics in the Film Community, 1930–1960* (Garden City, N.Y.: Doubleday, 1980), a supposedly thorough record, do *not* list West as on the Executive Board of the Screen Writer's Guild, app. 2, p. 436. They do list West as on "front" committees but categorize him as one of the "Liberals" in contrast to the supposed "Radicals" (apparently a quaint misnomer for Communist Party members), p. 437. While the whole study takes the Hollywood hacks and their Stalinist politics

both more earnestly and more blandly than any intelligent discussion should, it suggests some of the politics, and related information such as that in 1939 "the median wage for screenwriters was only 120" dollars a week; contrast West's three-to-four times that—or just note that West was making a dozen times more than the reasonable salary of thirty dollars a week he gives his studio artist Tod in *The Day of the Locust.*

7. I am quoting, as with all of West's novels, from *The Complete Works of Nathanael West* (New York, 1957), pp. 3–62. Because of many brief quotations from a short work, and because many readers will be using paperback reprints, further pagination is not given. The most detailed analysis, and a somewhat exaggerated evaluation, is provided by Gerald Locklin, *"The Dream of Balso Snell*: Journey into the Microcosm," in *Nathanael West: The Cheaters and the Cheated,* ed. David Madden (Deland, Fla., 1973), pp. 23–55. There are several suggestive points in Marcus Klein, "The Roots of Radical Experience in the Thirties," in *Proletarian Writers of the Thirties,* ed. David Madden (Carbondale: Southern Illinois Universal Press, 1968), pp. 142–45.

8. In an often rigorously informed discussion of sources (Huysmans, Cabell's *Jurgen,* Anatole France, etc.), Randall Reid puzzlingly treats Balso as "middle-aged" and translates the name as "asshole smell" (*Nathanael West, No Redeemer, No Promised Land* [Chicago, 1967]), pp. 16, 38). While I find Reid sometimes suggestive (though "running balls" might be a better connotation for the journeying adolescent), and agree with his point that West's "role of triumphant comedian was an unsuccessful impersonation," my emphasis generally differs.

9. Leslie A. Fiedler interprets this passage as West's dismissal of his Jewishness (which of course it isn't), though he was functioning as the first legion of the "take-over by Jewish American writers of the American imagination" ("Master of Drama," *Partisan Review* 34 [Summer 1967], 347–48).

10. For discussion of West's use of "surrealist art of incongruity" as part of the attack on art, see Victor Comerchero, *Nathanael West, The Ironic Prophet* (Syracuse, 1964), pp. 56 ff. There are other discussions of this influence, such as the parallels given by Robert I. Edenbaum, "Dada and Surrealism in the United States: A Literary

Instance," *Arts in Society* 5 (1968): 114–25. If one were to pursue the subject, it would be appropriate to look at images in artists that West was influenced by, such as Kurt Schwitters and Max Ernst.

11. It may not be altogether incidental that the first line West quotes from his novella in a publisher's advertisement which he apparently wrote was "O Anon! O Onan!" "Through the Hole in the Mundane Millstone" (1931), reprinted in the appendix to William White, *Nathanael West: A Comprehensive Bibliography* (Kent, Ohio, 1975), pp. 129–31. One might also relate his final metaphoric quote (not from the novella) to the same theme, Kurt Schwitters, *"Tout ce que l'artists crache, c'est l'art...."* Another insistent West point in this piece is his identifying not with bland American humor but with its modernist European antithesis—an issue I will return to in my concluding chapter.

Chapter Two

1. *Miss Lonelyhearts* in *The Complete Works of Nathanael West* (New York, 1957), pp. 63–140. For West's periodical versions of some of the chapters, see the primary bibliography, below, and for comparison with the books, see Carter A. Daniel, "West's Revisions of *Miss Lonelyhearts*," *Studies in Bibliography* 16 (1963): 232–43.

2. I am not, of course, suggesting that all homosexualities are pathological. As my colleague Karl Keller expertly points out, the Lonelyhearts problem is less homosexuality than the denial of it. The homosexuality issues have been much disputed in the criticism. Early on, Stanley Edgar Hyman made a more or less traditional Freudian diagnosis of Lonelyhearts's Oedipal condition, *Nathanael West* (Minneapolis, 1962), pp. 22–23. Victor Comerchero extended this in *Nathanael West, The Ironic Prophet*, pp. 84 ff. Randall Reid caught them out in overreadings (after all, we have almost nothing about the protagonist's early life), but in throwing out the critics' Freudian literalism he also foolishly threw out the crucial sexual ambivalence (*The Fiction of Nathaniel West*, pp. 73 ff). Others have followed Reid in denying the obvious, such as Miles D. Orvell, "The Messianic Sexuality of Miss Lonelyhearts," *Studies in Short Fiction* 10 (Spring 1973): 159–67. The fullest discussion is James W. Hickey, "Freudian Criticism and *Miss Lonelyhearts*," in *Nathanael West*, ed. David Madden, pp. 111–50. While he makes some interesting points, he

essentially reduces the figure to an "hysteric-schizophrenic"; this undermining of larger human relevance in the art is, of course, characteristic of thorough-going Freudian criticism. Perhaps most importantly, Lonelyhearts's sexual ambivalence takes sado-masochistic displacements, including Christianity.

3. I am here elaborating the doubleness I noted in an earlier essay (1967). West, in "Some Notes on Miss L" (1933), had defined the fiction as "the portrait of a priest of our time who has a religious experience. His case is classical and is built on all the cases in James's *Varieties of Religious Experience* and Starbuck's *Psychology of Religion*" (reprinted in White, *Nathanael West*, p. 166). I suspect that West was defending himself against his protagonist being taken as a mere freak. The saint/psychotic doubleness is spelled out in terms of the sources (primarily James) by Marcus Smith, "Religious Experience in *Miss Lonelyhearts*," *Contemporary Literature* 9 (Spring 1968): 172–88. On the other hand, there are those, from James Light on, who ignore the pathological and take the Christianity too literally, such as Thomas M. Lorch declaring that Lonelyhearts "goes to his death in the fullness of Christian faith, charity and hope" ("Religion and Art in *Miss Lonelyhearts*," *Renascence* 20 [Autumn 1967]: 13). See also his "West's *Miss Lonelyhearts*: Skepticism Mitigated?" *Renascence* 18 (Winter 1966): 99–109, which dismisses West's mockery of Catholic mysticism (as in the opening Shrike parody prayer using Loyola's "Spiritual Exercises") and also denies the Jamesian influence. Little better, of course, are readings which take a purely pathological emphasis, as in Gerald B. Nelson's erroneous and hyped-up "Lonelyhearts," in *Ten Versions of America* (New York, 1972), pp. 77–90. Others have more sensibly taken some double view of the protagonist, within the atheistic context, as with Mike Frank, "The Passion of Miss Lonelyhearts According to Nathanael West," *Studies in Short Fiction* 10 (Winter 1973): 67–73. There are some good comments on the human incompleteness of all the characters and the resulting manias in Roger D. Abrahams, "Androgynes Bound: Nathanael West's *Miss Lonelyhearts*," in *Seven Contemporary Authors*, ed. Thomas B. Whitbread (Austin, 1966), pp. 49–72.

4. I analyzed *Notes from Underground*, and also related it to the Lonelyhearts atheistic analogue, in my *Edges of Extremity: Some Problems of Literary Modernism* (Tulsa, Okla., 1980).

5. West's double plays on "order" are also sometimes misunder-

stood. Robert D. Richards, Jr., thinks that West is praising the desire
for order when he is exposing it as a compulsion in a universe lacking
any human, and humane, order ("Miss Lonelyhearts," *University
Review* 33 [December 1966]: 151–57).

6. I am suggesting a word change for West here; my researches
indicate that in the 1930s, as well as the present, Christian hysterics
did not chant "Christ" or "Jesus Christ," as West has it, but the more
personal (and erotic?) "Jesus." Is this a Jewish slip? Some of West's
aslant Jewishness appears in the pastoral chapter where the man at
the "Aw-Kum-On Garage" in rural Connecticut "said there was still
plenty of deer at the pond because no yids ever went there. He said
it wasn't the hunters who drove out the deer but the yids." Some
displaced mocking Jewish touches may include *shiksa* Betty's belief
in therapeutic soup and the fearful fascination with Christian lunacy.

7. Many critical discussions overdo the wickedness of Shrike,
though he is but a pathetic and hysterical alter ego of Lonelyhearts
(speeches given to Shrike were originally given to Lonelyhearts in the
earlier versions published as periodical stories). In the overall Westean
pattern, Shrike stands as one of a series of faltering verbal-sadistic
clowns, a masquerader gone compulsive. J. A. Ward suggests that
Shrike derives from Groucho Marx, for whom West's brother-in-law
Perelman wrote scripts ("The Hollywood Metaphor: The Marx
Brothers, S. J. Perelman, and Nathanael West," *Southern Review* 12
(July 1976): 659–72). Mary Shrike may also be viewed as a painfully
comic automation in her fantasy spiels, sexual teases, and "mechanical"
appearance (a "tight, shiny dress that was like glass-covered steel"),
a parody mechanism of lascivious frigidity.

8. West's urban "waste land" is even more barren than the more
"optimistic" one of Eliot's poem suggested Edmond L. Volpe in a
series of loose comparisons ("The Waste Land of Nathanael West,"
Renascence 13 (1961): 61–77). Incidentally, Volpe interprets the
two narrative shifts away from the protagonist as a faltering in West's
feelings, but I think they may be more simply explainable as somewhat
awkward plot devices used to reinforce the ironic failures of com-
munication.

9. In a brief piece written in the same period, West insists "In
America violence is idiomatic." Much ahead of the more general
consciousness of the centrality of violence to the American psyche,
he simply refers it to our realities and our media fare ("Some Notes

on Violence" (1933), reprinted in White, *Nathanael West*, pp. 162–64). For a detailed discussion of the psychodrama of violence with Lonelyhearts, with repressed sensory responses leading to aimless aggression which becomes regressive self-destruction, see Lawrence DiStasi, "Aggression in Miss Lonelyhearts: Nowhere to Throw the Stone," *Nathanael West*, ed. Madden, pp. 83–101. He informed me that the argument could be understood as a Marcusean dialectic about pseudo-sublimation in a deceitfully controlling cultural order.

Chapter Three

1. *A Cool Million* in *The Complete Works of Nathanael West*, pp. 141–255. There seems to be a consensus among the better critics that this work, in its stylistic flatness, heavy-handed mockeries, and melodramatic crudity, adds up to something "hardly worthy of sustained comment" (Comerchero, p. 103). In contrast, see the typically obtuse judgment of R. W. B. Lewis that "the perspective in *A Cool Million* is exactly right" ("Days of Wrath and Anger," in *Trials of the Word* [New Haven, 1965], p. 215). Douglas Shepard lays out the major literary source in "Nathanael West Rewrites Horatio Alger," *Satire News Letter* 3 (Fall 1965): 13–28.

2. Some of West's usual anti-Jewishness appears along with satire of populist anti-Semitism ("Jewish international bankers"). Thus one Asa Goldstein is "cause of the tragedy" of the foreclosure on the Pitkin place because he will unscrupulously do anything to get it for his antique business. In another episode, Lem is in jail and his court-appointed attorney, Seth Abromowitz, "a small man of the Jewish persuasion," appears; his first question: " 'Have you any money?' said this member of the chosen people." Later, "showing his true colors," he insults, threatens, and tries to cheat Lem. There may also be some parody-allusions with Jewish reference, as in dictator Shagpoke's rhetorical question on martyr Pitkin Day: "Why are we celebrating this day above other days?" (Compare the opening question from the Haggadah for the Jewish Passover celebration of freedom: "Why is this day different than other days?"

3. Shagpoke may be West's double play around a money chaser of dubious competence (shag: run, chase; poke: bag, wallet, slow). In the academic criticism there appears considerable gaming about West's names, often to the detriment of deeper perception. Thus

Nathan Whipple is a "whipped version" of Nathan Weinstein (West). Lemuel, of course, is the first name of Swift's Gulliver. Pitkin may be the common colonial name (institutionalized, I recall, in street names in several places and a county in Colorado). Betty, as used here, must simply be the stock girlish figure (also used in *Miss Lonely-hearts* for the most conventional female), though Prail could be a wordplay (frail-pail?—she certainly gets knocked over and dumped in often enough). But West shows little allegorical cast of mind and is not very ingenious in his use of names. Samuel Perkins, for little reason, applies to a minor character here though also used for the all-smelling biographer in *Balso Snell*. Stock Irish, Chinese, Jewish, and other, names appear simply for stock effects. Some are crudely jokey: Sylvanus Snodgrasse for the unnatural poet; Chin Lao Tse, an unphilosophical whorehouse thug; early American Zackery Coates for a "Storm Trooper." Israel Satinpenny, educated Indian chief and prophet of decadence, may combine the jokey and a slight reference to the myth of the Indians as a lost tribe of Israelites. In spite of portentous exegetes, Jake Raven for another Indian is probably no more than the slight tonal incongruity it appears to be. To get ornately allegorical with such material is a literary criticism fallacy of misplaced concreteness.

4. The Pike County man may also be a heavy satire of the Davy Crockett frontier type, and more generally of Western humor—West's recurrently expressed distaste for traditional American humor. For details on the former, but not the later, point, see David D. Galloway, "A Picaresque Apprenticeship: Nathanael West's *The Dream Life of Balso Snell* and *A Cool Million*," *Wisconsin Studies in Contemporary Literature* 5 (Summer 1964): 110–26.

5. Randall Reid points to several possible personal "allusions" that "suggest that West's attitude towards his materials may have been muddled by irrelevant motives" (*The Fiction of Nathanael West*, p. 110).

6. Most political commentators do not question the political issue, as I do here, and later. Joseph Blotner presents a bland summary of *A Cool Million* as expressive of a "growing concern with native Fascism" (*The Modern American Political Novel, 1900–1960* [Austin: University of Texas Press, 1966]), pp. 244–47. Nor does Daniel Aaron question the political theme on linking this fiction with recent savage historical farces by Coover, Roth, and others. Frequently

"the writer will present his Waste-land in the form of black farce as Nathanael West did in his lunatic novel of the 1930s ... a burlesque of American wouldbe Hitlers and on the hypocrisy of the American gospel of success." While West's subject and manner appear considerably different than the 1970s farceurs, they may be linked on the general point that "history becomes nightmare" ("Fictionalizing the Past," *Partisan Review* 42, no. 2 (1980): 231–32).

Chapter Four

1. *The Day of the Locust* in *The Complete Works of Nathanael West*, pp. 256–421. Probably the central biblical source for the entitling metaphor is Revelation, 9:3–4 (KJV): "And there came out of the smoke locusts upon the earth: and unto them was given power, as the scorpions of the earth have power. And it was commanded them that they should not hurt the grass of the earth, neither any tree; but only those men which have not the seal of God in their foreheads." Robert Alter surveys briefly some of the Jewish tradition of apocalypse and loosely relates it to West's novel, though he weirdly thinks the book is about Homer (and that he should be compared unfavorably to Leonard Bast in *Howard's End*). "The Apocalyptic Temper," *Commentary* 41 (June 1966): 61–66.

2. For a comparison of West's motifs with other Hollywood fictions, see my "The Hollywood Image," *Coastlines* 5 (1961): 17–27, and "The Last Masquerade," in *Nathanael West*, ed. David Madden pp. 179–93. In recent years, there have been a number of studies of West's novel in the context of the Hollywood subgenre. A weak one vaguely relating West's to American Dream longings is Jonas Spatz, *Hollywood in Fiction* (The Hague, 1969), pp. 133–41. A much better one, apt on the sexual detail and role-playing, is Walter Wells, "Shriek of the Locusts," in *Tycoons and Locusts: A Regional Look at Hollywood Fictions of the 1930s* (Carbondale, 1973), pp. 49–70. In one of the best such discussions, Carolyn See points out about the type generally the predominance of the theme that *"You are what you pretend to be"* ("The Hollywood Novel: The American Dream Cheats," in *Tough Guy Writers of the Thirties,* ed. David Madden [Carbondale: Southern Illinois University Press, 1968], pp. 199–217).

3. Difficulties with Tod have often been reported, as early on by Edmund Wilson, "The Boys in the Back Room" (1941), in *A Lit-*

erary Chronicle, 1920–1950 (New York, 1956), pp. 245–49; by Stanley Edgar Hyman, *Nathanael West* (Minneapolis, 1962), p. 33. and by Pauline Kael, about the book as well as the not very successful John Schlesinger movie version of *The Day of the Locust* (1975), "The Darned," in *Reeling* (New York, 1976), pp. 272–78. While I think Kael's remarks on the movie are one of the most acute discussions of it, the comments on the novel seem patronizingly bigoted.

4. The masquerading point can get weirdly twisted around; A. M. Tibbets insisted that "the book is a dance of masks, only," which obscurely senses the theme but dismisses it for a foolishly narrow standard of realism in his polemic against West ("The Strange Half-World of Nathanael West," *Prarie Schooner* 34 [Spring 1960]: 8–14). A better sense of West's insistent realism appears in Daniel R. Brown, "The War Within Nathanael West: Naturalism and Existentialism," *Modern Fiction Studies* 20 (Summer 1974): 181–202. R. W. B. Lewis, in surveying the typology, quite misses the point of Harry's masqueraded clowning by seeing it as positive ("The Aspiring Clown," *Learners and Discerners*, ed. Robert E. Scholes [Charlottesville: University of Virginia Press, 1964], pp. 103–4).

5. There have been a number of discussions of Faye as American bitch and destructive female, often rather love-hating (that is, Norman Mailer-ish) by male critics, though perhaps not enough emphasis on the obvious—as a machined masturbatory image and nonperson consumer in her fantasy role. See Leslie Fiedler, *Love and Death in the American Novel* (New York: Criterion, 1960), pp. 316–18, 461–66. He may overemphasize the self-consciously satiric element, as he does elsewhere in his comment on cowboy-actor Earl as "travesty in full malice of the Westerner" (*The Return of the Vanishing American* [New York: Stein and Day, 1968], p. 149).

6. If not Claude directly, certainly his party provides a focus for West's anti-Jewish mockeries, including of the "illiterate mockies" who were Hollywood producers. More jokey are such bits as an Indian bit player, Chief Kiss-My-Towkus (Yiddish for ass). Note also that the theater where the riot takes place is "Kahn's Persian Palace" (Grauman's Chinese cinema palace of the time), and its sign—a take-off on Coleridge, Yiddish syntax, and perhaps a Coney Island movie house—reads "Mr. Kahn a Pleasure Dome Decreed." Earlier, West has written a brief sarcastic burlesque about a Jewish producer and writer one-upping each other: "Business Deal" (*Americana* [1933]),

reprinted in White, *Nathanael West: A Comprehensive Bibliography*, pp. 167–70. The Jewish motifs in West are insistent, and clowningly negative.

7. Victor Comerchero rightly noted, though his chapter on the novel is rather weak, that "Homer becomes a symbolic abstraction of the crowd" (*Nathanael West, The Ironic Prophet*, p. 137).

8. William Van O'Connor noted (no doubt because of some of the characterization of Homer) West's typological relation to Sherwood Anderson (*The Grotesque, and Other Essays* [Carbondale: Southern Illinois University Press, 1962], p. 8). Randall Reid provides the most detailed discussion of West's relation to Sherwood Anderson's writings (*The Fiction of Nathanael West*, pp. 139–50). But he oddly fails to note the masturbatory emphasis, a recurring one in West.

9. The use of music in the novel is suggestively discussed by Reid, above, and by Robert I. Edenbaum, "From American Dream to Pavlovian Nightmare," in *Nathanael West*, ed. Madden, pp. 201–16. Both see the music, as with the Bach at Harry's funeral emphasizing compassion. The only discussion of the painting allusions is the rather heavy-handed one of Donald T. Torchiana, "*The Day of the Locust* and the Painter's Eye," in *Nathanael West*, ed. Madden, pp. 249–82, to which I am indebted for the identification of the Janvier allusion, p. 275.

10. Some of the source material, though not my interpretation, can be found in Jay Martin's *Nathanael West, The Art of His Life* (New York, 1970): letters on "progressive" politics to Malcolm Cowley and Jack Conroy in 1938 are quoted on pp. 335–36. Background studies given by Martin include Daniel Aaron, *Writers On the Left* (New York, 1961), who I think underrates West's leftism, and Murray Kempton, *Part of Our Time* (New York, 1955), who never quite makes the politics clear. See also my discussion in the biographical section of chapter 1, above. Max F. Schulz makes the commonsensical point that "strong" leftist politics "characterize West's novels as sincere expression of their time" (I suspect some role-playing), and resulted in fictions sometimes "more heated and polemical than is good for them" ("Nathanael West's Desperate Detachment," *Radical Sophistication, Studies in Contemporary Jewish American Novelists* [Athens, Ohio, 1969], pp. 53–54). Most critics on West tend to naively ignore or else downplay, whether out of ignorance or misplaced "tolerance," West's "progressive" politics.

Chapter Five

1. Besides works by and about West (cited elsewhere in this study), and standard American authors, writings alluded to in this section include: Ivan Illich, *Toward a History of Needs*; Aldous Huxley, *Collected Essays*; Alexis de Toqueville, *Democracy in America*, vol. 2; Jose Ortega y Gasset, *The Revolt of the Masses*; Soren Kierkegaard, *The Present Age*; Denis Brogan, *The American Character*; Jean-Paul Sartre, *Selected Essays*; the sociological essays of Robert Balah on "civic religion"; Robert Heilbroner, *An Inquiry into the Human Prospect*; Frederick Nietzsche, *The Will to Power*; D. H. Lawrence, *Studies in Classic American Literature*; Terence des Pres, *The Survivors*; Kingsley Widmer, "In Praise of Waste: Reflections On Contemporary Culture," *Partisan Review* (1979), and "Sensibility Under Technocracy," *Human Connection and the New Media*, ed. B. Schwartz (Englewood Cliffs, N.J., Prentice-Hall, 1973).

2. "Euripides—A Playwright," (*Casements* [1923], reprinted in White, *Nathaniel West*, pp. 120–23).

3. For a few examples of the evidence of West's influence, see the citations in *The Habit of Being: Letters of Flannery O'Connor* (New York: Knopf, 1979), and her relation to West discussed by Frederick J. Hoffman, "The Search for Redemption," *The Added Dimension: Flannery O'Connor*, ed. Melvin J. Friedman and L. A. Lawson (New York: New York University Press, 1966); John Hawkes linked O'Connor, West, and himself in "Flannery O'Connor's Devil," *Sewanee Review* 70 (Summer 1962): 395–407; Leslie Fiedler suggested that Jeremy Lerner's *Drive, He Said* came out of West, "The Two Memories, Reflections on Writers and Writings in the Thirties," in *Proletarian Writers of the Thirties*, ed. David Madden (Carbondale: Southern Illinois University Press, 1968); others have linked such equally synthetic fictionists as Bruce Jay Friedman with West; James Light lists some of those mentioned above, plus Edward Lewis Wallant (*The Children*), *Nathaniel West: An Interpretative Study* (Evanston, 1961), pp. 211–13; a number of discussions see West's mockeries as a source of the American version of "black humor," as does Brom Weber, "The Mode of 'Black Humor,' " in *The Comic Imagination in American Literature*, ed. Louis D. Rubin, Jr. (New Brunswick, N.J.: Rutgers University Press, 1973), p. 366, though one has to be doubtful about all the influence he attributes to *The*

Dream Life of Balso Snell; for Paul Goodman, see his several comments on West in his *Utopian Essays* (1961), and for Norman Mailer, his comments on, and adaption of, West in the Las Vegas scene, in *Armies of the Night* (1968); for an especially Jewish role and influence, see many of the discussions cited earlier (Schulz, Donald, and Fiedler). There is much more, but the summation point should be that the fiction of Nathanael West have become a recognized part of the American cultural furnishings.

4. If I may be indulged in two summary anecdotes (from an earlier essay of mine on *The Day of the Locust*), perhaps I can suggest a personal dimension to the Westean insights.

(1) "Alone and despairing in Los Angeles one New Year's Eve a generation ago [the mid–1940s], I drifted about downtown. So did thousands of other young, and not so young, inadequately narcoticized delinquents. The aimlessly circling crowd grew, clotted here and there around a curse that offered a fight or a scream that suggested a rape. There were random bits of violence, several plate-glass windows shattered, many dresses furtively torn, a few arrests, a few injuries, but finally nothing, not even an adequate mob scene, could find its form. We were all avid spectators for some image of a promising end but all cheated of even the hysteria for which we longed."

(2) "As I understand West's masquerade, it is no mere metaphor. A decade after West's novel ... I washed up in those same brightly stagnant purlieus. A self-identified writer with some naively larcenous Hollywood ambitions, I temporarily played the role of free-lance advertising hack, market researcher, and whatever other surrogate arts with which I could connivingly connect. However, I kept up the payments on my new car by pretending a more utilitarian craft, template-maker in a Santa Monica aircraft factory neatly triangulated between my Malibu beach rental and Hollywood. By making metal patterns all night (the graveyard shift) and by foregoing the usual ways of dreaming (asleep), I could afford being a not very successful Hollywood self-promoter during the day and an artist-pretender during the evening: a multiple imitation-person.

"Eventually, I discovered that many of my co-workers were also masquerading: an actress pretending to be a time-clerk, an assistant director playing at jig-building, a cameraman hobbying with airframe blueprints, an actor practicing a quaint scene in the tool crib. My benchmate was also a writer, disguised, he explained, as a cam-maker

in order to accumulate naturalistic detail for scenarios. Not everyone
in the shop seemed to be a counterfeiter. At the next bench, for salutary example, was a scruffily dressed and taciturn middle-aged working
man who spent his breaks studying the racing results in the paper.
At least, I thought, this sad little tool-maker dreaming of long-shots
was for real—until I bumped into him one afternoon as he got out
of a new Cadillac in front of one of Beverly Hills' most expensive
bistros. As a gesture of noblesse to my peasant shock, he removed his
homburg, waved me in past the obsequious headwaiter and, over a
double of the best cognac which I imitatingly ordered, he gave me
to know that he was a bigtime professional gambler, temporarily
forced to counterfeit a trivial trade so to display a "visible means of
support" to the legal guardians. Just how much of this was costuming
I had no way of knowing. And probably, to make a Westean point,
he didn't either.

"Such imitation lives, like screen images, are often cleverly quick-
cut; the gambler-template-maker soon disappeared. His benchmate,
who turned out to be a sometime war-hero and actor with alimony
problems, could provide no enlightenment. Perhaps the horseplayer
had yet other masquerades to template. Or even, perhaps, like myself,
he finally understood the point of my farmer-grandfather's warning
that 'ta sell corn ya got ta have corn,' and gave up Hollywood
ambitions.

"From my experience, then, I see Nathanael West as a sharply sad-
eyed documentor of a particular reality . . . though of course there is
much else. . . ."

Selected Bibliography

PRIMARY SOURCES

The Complete Works of Nathanael West. New York: Farrar, Straus, Cudahy, 1957. Reprint. New York: Octagon Books of Farrar, Straus and Giroux, 1980.

The Dream of Life of Balso Snell. New York and Paris: Contact Editions, 1931. Reprint. *The Dream Life of Balso Snell/A Cool Million.* New York: Farrar, Straus and Giroux Paperback, 1979.

Miss Lonelyhearts. New York: Liveright, 1933. Reprint. *Miss Lonelyhearts and The Day of the Locust.* New York: New Directions Paperback, 1962.

A Cool Million, The Dismantling of Lemuel Pitkin. New York: Covici, Friede, 1934. Reprint. *The Dream Life of Balso Snell/ A Cool Million.* New York: Farrar, Straus and Giroux Paperback, 1979.

The Day of the Locust. New York: Random House, 1939. Reprint. *Miss Lonelyhearts and The Day of the Locust.* New York: New Directions Paperback, 1962.

The following brief works are all of those that West published in periodicals; except for those that West revised for *Miss Lonelyhearts* and *The Day of the Locust*, they are slight; all are reprinted in "Appendix: Uncollected Writings of Nathanael West," in *Nathanael West: A Comprehensive Bibliography*, by William White (Kent, Ohio: Kent State University Press, 1975), pp. 119–80). The order is chronological; original publication data are included.

"Rondeau." *The Brown Jug,* December 1922, p. 24.
"Euripides—A Playwright." *Casements* 1 (July 1923): 2–4.
"Death." *Casements* 2 (May 1924): 15.
"A Barefaced Lie." *Overland Monthly* 87 (July 1929): 210, 219.
"Miss Lonelyhearts and the Lamb." *Contact* 1 (February 1932): 80–85.

"Miss Lonelyhearts and the Dead Pan." *Contact* 1 (May 1932): 13–21.
"Miss Lonelyhearts and the Clean Old Man." *Contact* 1 (May 1932): 22–27.
"Miss Lonelyhearts in the Dismal Swamp." *Contempo* 2 (5 July, 1932): 1–2.
"Miss Lonelyhearts on a Field Trip." *Contact* 1 (October 1932): 50–57.
"Some Notes on Violence." *Contact* 1 (October 1932): 132–3.
"Christmas Poem." *Contempo* 3 (February 21, 1933): 14.
"Some Notes on Miss L." *Contempo* 3 (May 13, 1933): 1–2.
"Business Deal." *Americana* 1 (October 1933): 14–15.
"Soft Soap for the Barber." *New Republic* 81 (14 November, 1934): 23.
"Bird and Bottle." *Pacific Weekly* 5 (10 November, 1936): 329–31.

SECONDARY SOURCES

1. Bibliographies
Vannatta, Dennis P. *Nathanael West: An Annotated Bibliography of the Scholarship and Works.* New York: Garland Publishing, 1976. A fulsome compilation, including many merely passing references, with annotations, under an elaborate set of rubrics, which must be treated with considerable skepticism.
White, William. *Nathanael West: A Comprehensive Bibliography.* Kent, Ohio: Kent State University Press, 1975. The fullest of his many West bibliographies.

2. Biographies
Light, James F. *Nathanael West, An Interpretative Study.* 2d ed. Evanston, Ill.: Northwestern University Press, 1971. This first (1961) scholarly book on the subject gives considerable and thoughtful biographical material. The interpretations of West's fiction are sometimes marred by Jungian and other vagaries. The second edition adds a sketchy preface about a few other studies.
Martin Jay. *Nathanael West, The Art of His Life.* New York: Farrar, Straus and Giroux, 1970. A large and fulsome biography, arduously done and informative on many matters, it includes sum-

maries of West's unpublished writings and movie scripts. It corrects earlier accounts, such as Light's. Some of the writing is pompously inflated and the interpretations of the life and the writings are often uninsightful.

3. Books and pamphlets

Comerchero, Victor. *Nathanael West, The Ironic Prophet.* Syracuse, N.Y.: Syracuse University Press, 1964. An intelligent and often suggestive detailed analysis of Freudian and mythic motifs in West's fiction, it is weak on a coherent interpretation of the individual novels.

Cramer, Carter M. *The World of Nathanael West.* Emporia, Kansas: Emporia State Research Studies, 1971. Earnest paraphrases to show West's mixed forms, it is marked by a moralistic distaste.

Hyman, Stanley Edgar. *Nathanael West.* Minneapolis: University of Minnesota Press, 1962. This introductory essay is brief but often acute; it raised issues, such as Freudian interpretations, pursued by later critics.

Malin, Irving. *Nathananael West's Novels.* Carbondale: Southern Illinois University Press, 1972. This unhelpful exercise is mostly an overreading of secondary metaphors in an earnest parody of symbolist mannerisms. It is also poorly informed.

Perry, Robert M. *Nathanael West's Miss Lonelyhearts.* New York: Seabury Press, 1969. A trite and simple minded Protestant-Christian homily.

Reid, Randall. *The Fiction of Nathanael West, No Redeemer, No Promised Land.* Chicago: University of Chicago Press, 1967. Though old-fashioned in focus, this rigorous and ranging discussion of West's literary sources also makes many apt critical points around the theme of West as a prophet of decadence.

Scott, Nathan A., Jr. *Nathanael West.* Grand Rapids, Mich.: William B. Eerdmans Publishing, 1971. An introductory essay, this stock summary and paraphrase provides little critical or other insight.

4. Chapters and articles

Aaron, Daniel. "Late Thoughts on Nathanael West." *Massachusetts Review* 6 (Spring 1965): 307–16. Notes on the William Jamesian emphasis in *Miss Lonelyhearts* and on the beyond-politics emphasis in *A Cool Million.*

Abrahams, Roger D. "Androgynes Bound: Nathanael West's *Miss Lonelyhearts*." In *Seven Contemporary Authors*, edited by Thomas B. Whitbread, pp. 49–72. Austin: University of Texas Press, 1966. A nondoctrinaire psychological analysis of characters in the Lonelyhearts pattern. Suggestive.

Andreach, Robert J. "Nathanael West's Miss Lonelyhearts: Between the Dead Pan and the Unborn Christ." *Modern Fiction Studies* 12 (Summer 1966):251–60. Ingenious allegorical reading with Shrike as god Pan but no Christ, yet.

Apple, Max. "History and Case History in *Red Cavalry* and *The Day of the Locust*." In *Nathanael West: The Cheaters and the Cheated*, edited by David Madden, pp. 235–47. Deland, Fla.: Everett/Edwards, 1973. Mostly arbitrary, and pretentious, comparisons between Isaac Babel's Russian Civil War sketches and West's last novel.

Auden, W. H. "West's Disease." *The Dyer's Hand*. New York: Random House, 1962, pp. 238–45. Disapproving comments on West's fictionalizing the "disease" of "wish" fantasies—sophisticated Christian moralizing.

Bowden, James H. "No Redactor, No Reward." In *Nathanael West: The Cheaters and the Cheated*, edited by David Madden, pp. 283–97. Deland, Fla.: Everett/Edwards, 1973. Lively and suggestive religious reflections on West's atheistic writings, utilizing Ecclesiastes.

Brand, John M. "A Word Is a Word Is a Word." In *Nathanael West: The Cheaters and the Cheated*, edited by David Madden, pp. 57–75. Deland, Fla.: Everett/Edwards, 1973. Ponderous comparisons of biblical prophets and *The Dream Life of Balso Snell*.

Brown, Daniel R. "The War Within Nathanael West: Naturalism and Existentialism." *Modern Fiction Studies* 20 (Summer 1974): 181–202. This comparative study emphasizes West's combination of realism and existential grotesquery.

Clarke, Bruce. "Miss Lonelyhearts and the Detached Consciousness." *Paunch* 42–3 (December 1975):21–39. A dogmatic sexual theorizing which projects Betty as life-affirmative.

Coates, Robert M. Introduction to *Miss Lonelyhearts*. New York: New Directions, 1946, pp. 1–7. An early and influential introduction emphasizing West's literary artistry.

Daniel, Carter A. "West's Revisions of *Miss Lonelyhearts*." *Studies in Bibliography* 16 (1963): 232–43. This compares the five pieces in periodicals with the final published book version.

Dardis, Tom. "Nathanael West: The Scavenger of the Back Lots." In *Some Time in the Sun*. New York: Scribners, 1976, pp. 151–81. A not very perceptive rehash of West's role as a Hollywood script writer.

DiStasi, Lawrence W. "Aggression in *Miss Lonelyhearts*: Nowhere to Throw the Stone." In *Nathanael West: The Cheaters and the Cheated*, edited by David Madden, pp. 83–101. Deland, Fla.: Everett/Edwards, 1973. A left-Freudian analysis of the violence and self-destructiveness, heavy but sometimes suggestive.

Donald, Miles. *The American Novel in the Twentieth Century*. New York: Doubleday, 1978, pp. 162–66. Loosely argues that West's self-doubting irony was especially Jewish in heritage.

Edenbaum, Robert I. "Dada and Surrealism in the United States: A Literary Instance." *Arts in Society* 5 (1968): 114–25. A slight account of some dada and surrealist parallels with West's fictions.

———. "From American Dream to Pavlovian Nightmare." In *Nathanael West: The Cheaters and the Cheated*, edited by David Madden, pp. 201–16. Deland, Fla.: Everett/Edwards, 1973. An explication of some of the tropes of *The Day of the Locust*, with a concluding emphasis on West's compassion for grotesques.

Frank, Mike. "The Passion of Miss Lonelyhearts According to Nathanael West." *Studies in Short Fiction* 10 (Winter 1973): 67–73. A succinct analysis properly emphasizing West's religious negativism.

Galloway, David D. "Nathanael West's Dream Dump." *Critique* 6 (Winter 1963): 46–64. Loosely and narrowly summarizes some interrelations, not very important, of the Hollywood fictions of Fitzgerald and West.

———. "A Picaresque Apprenticeship: Nathanael West's *The Dream Life of Balso Snell* and *A Cool Million*." *Wisconsin Studies in Contemporary Literature* 5 (Summer 1964): 110–26. An analysis of West's lesser fiction, most thoughtful on some cultural background for *A Cool Million*.

Geha, Richard. "*Miss Lonelyhearts*: A Dual Mission of Mercy." *Hartford Studies in Literature* 3 (1971): 116–31. A literal-minded psychoanalytic interpretation around the castration motif.

Gehman, Richard. Introduction to *The Day of the Locust*. New York: New Directions, 1950, pp. ix–xxiii. Historically influential essay emphasizing the life.

Herbst, Josephine. "Nathanael West." *Kenyon Review* 23 (Autumn 1961): 611–30. A fervent commentary by an early 1930s writer-friend of West's.

Kael, Pauline. "The Darned." In *Reeling*. Boston: Little, Brown, 1976, pp. 472–78. Apt comments on the John Schlesinger movie of *Locust* though inadequate view of West.

Hickey, James W. "Freudian Criticism and *Miss Lonelyhearts*." In *Nathanael West: The Cheaters and the Cheated*, edited by David Madden, pp. 111–50. Deland, Fla.: Everett/Edwards, 1973. The fullest detailed psychoanalytic interpretation, useful though still essentially reductive of the art and thought.

Jackson, Thomas H. Introduction to *Twentieth Century Interpretations of Miss Lonelyhearts*. Englewood Cliffs, N.J.: Prentice-Hall, 1971. An urbanely ill-focused summary of some issues around *Miss Lonelyhearts* which prefaces a mediocre collection of critical bits.

Kernan, Alvin B. "The Mob Tendency: *The Day of the Locust*." In *The Plot of Satire*. New Haven, Conn.: Yale University Press, 1965, pp. 66–88. A stock summary of the last novel which oddly views West as a conventional conservative satirist.

Klein, Marcus. "The Roots of Radical Experience in the Thirties." In *Proletarian Writers of the Thirties*, edited by David Madden, pp. 142–45. Carbondale: Southern Illinois University Press, 1968. Though not really related to the theme, some suggestive points on *The Dream Life of Balso Snell*.

Locklin, Gerald. "*The Dream Life of Balso Snell*: Journey into the Microcosm." In *Nathanael West: The Cheaters and the Cheated*, edited by David Madden, pp. 23–55. Deland, Fla.: Everett/Edwards, 1973. The fullest, most exacting, and somewhat exaggerated, analysis of West's first novella. Useful.

Lokke, V. L. "A Side Glance of Medusa: Hollywood, the Literature Boys, and Nathanael West." *Southwest Review* 46 (Winter 1961): 33–45. Gives West's insistently negative treatment of Hollywood symbology, in contrast to some other writers, as part of a pervasive attack on American mass culture.

Lorch, Thomas M. "West's *Miss Lonelyhearts*: Skepticism Mitigated?" *Renascence* 18 (Winter 1966): 99–109. See below.

_____. "Religion and Art in *Miss Lonelyhearts.*" *Renascence* 20 (Autumn 1967): 11–17. These two pieces provide an earnestly desperate misreading to affirm positive Christian values (mainline Catholic) in West.

May, John R. "Apocalyptic Judgment in Faulkner, West, and O'Connor." In *Toward a New Earth.* Notre Dame: University of Notre Dame Press, 1972, pp. 92–144. Summarizes *Miss Lonelyhearts* as protagonist's punishment for religious "presumption."

Mueller, Lavonne. "Malamud and West: Tyranny of the Dream Dump." In *Nathanael West: The Cheaters and the Cheated,* edited by David Madden, pp. 221–34. Deland, Fla.: Everett/Edwards, 1973. A series of loose analogies between Bernard Malamud's baseball fable, *The Natural,* and *The Day of the Locust.*

Nelson, Gerald B. "Lonelyhearts." In *Ten Versions of America.* New York: A. A. Knopf, 1972, pp. 77–90. Badly written and portentous misreadings of *Miss Lonelyhearts* as a documentation of pathology.

Orvell, Miles D. "The Messianic Sexuality in *Miss Lonelyhearts.*" *Studies in Short Fiction* 10 (Spring 1973): 159–67. A simple-minded argument against seeing the homosexuality and pathology in West's protagonist.

Olsen, Bruce. "Nathanael West, the Use of Cynicism." In *Minor American Novelists,* edited by Charles Alva Hoyt, pp. 81–94. Carbondale: Southern Illinois University Press, 1970. A discussion of role-playing West as an artistically faltering nihilist.

Perelman, S. J. "The Hindsight Saga." In *The Last Laugh.* New York: Simon and Schuster, 1981. Wry fragment of a memoir about West by his late brother-in-law.

Pinsker, Sanford. "Charles Dickens and Nathanael West; Great Expectations Unfulfilled." *Topic:* 18 9 (1969): 40–52. Loose comparisons of *Miss Lonelyhearts* with *Great Expectations* and *A Cool Million* with *Martin Chuzzlewit,* for no very good reason.

Podhoretz, Norman. "Nathanael West: A Particular Kind of Joking." In *Doings and Undoings: The Fifties and After in American Writing.* New York: Random House, 1964, pp. 65–75. A glib fashion-mongering long review (originally 1957) indicating West's changed status in a New York literary-publishing circle.

Ross, Alan. "The Dead Center: An Introduction to Nathanael West." In *The Complete Works of Nathanael West.* New York: Farrar, 1957, pp. vii–xxii. An influential positive essay, which encouraged West's heightened reputation, by a British critic who emphasized social history.

Schulz, Max F. "Nathanael West's Desperate Detachment." In *Radical Sophistication, Studies in Contemporary Jewish American Novelists*. Athens: Ohio University Press, 1969, pp. 36–55. Thoughtfully argues that West's anger against a bad American society defeated his art but provided an important legacy for later Jewish novelists.

Shelton, Frank W. "Nathanael West and the Theatre of the Absurd: A Comparative Study." *Southern Humanities Review* 10 (Summer 1976): 225–34. Catalogs some simple similarities of theme in West's fictions and some absurdist dramas, with the major point that they reflected the times.

Simonson, Harold P. "California, Nathanael West, and the Journey's End." In *The Closed Frontier*. New York: Knopf, 1970, pp. 99–124. This summary of all the book fiction emphasizes the last as the negative ending of the American Western dream.

Smith, Marcus. "Religious Experience in *Miss Lonelyhearts*." *Contemporary Literature* 9 (Spring 1968): 172–88. The major part is a detailed analysis of West's acknowledged use of William James's *Variety of Religious Experience*.

———. "The Crucial Departure: Irony and Point-of-View in *Miss Lonelyhearts*." *Nathanael West: The Cheated and the Cheaters*, edited by David Madden, pp. 103–10. Deland, Fla.: Everett/Edwards, 1973. A note on the mixture of irony and sympathy in the technique of West's presentation of his central character.

Spatz, Jonas. *Hollywood in Fiction*. The Hague: Mouton, 1969. Pp. 133–41. Vaguely and confusedly relates West's fiction to American utopian longings.

Steiner, T. R. "West's Lemuel and the American Dream." *Nathanael West: The Cheaters and the Cheated*, edited by David Madden, pp. 157–70. Deland, Fla.: Everett/Edwards, 1973. Somewhat pompous ruminations about, and Jewish associations with, *A Cool Million*.

Swingewood, Alan. "Alienation, Reification, and the Novel: Sartre, Camus, Nathanael West." In *The Sociology of Literature*. London: 1972, pp. 237–45 (on West). From a clichéd Marxist perspective, a poorly informed and imperceptive summary of *Miss Lonelyhearts* as a portrayal of social alienation.

Symons, Julian. "The Case of Nathanael West." In *Critical Occasions*.

London: Routledge, 1966, pp. 99–105. A brief and rather obtuse polemic against West for being an inadequate artist of only personal despair.

Tibbetts, A. M. "The Strange Half-World of Nathanael West." *Prarie Schooner* 34 (Spring 1960): 8–14. A polemic against West for his supposed inadequacy at commonplace realism.

Torchiana, Donald T. "*The Day of the Locust* and the Painter's Eye." In *Nathanael West: The Cheaters and the Cheated*, edited by David Madden, pp. 249–82. Deland, Fla.: Everett/Edwards, 1973. Specific but often exaggerated analogues in grotesque paintings, following out the allusions in *The Day of the Locust*.

Tropp, Martin. "Nathanael West and the Persistence of Hope." *Renascence* 31 (Summer 1979):205–14. A few metaphors suggest some stock positive faith and love in West.

Wadlington, Warwick. "Nathanael West and the Confidence Game." In *Nathanael West: The Cheaters and the Cheated*, edited by David Madden, pp. 299–322. Deland, Fla.: Everett/Edwards, 1973. Some analysis of West as continuing an ironic mode belonging to earlier American authors (ignoring his European roots), with the artist as con man, however unconfident in his case.

Ward, J. A. "The Hollywood Metaphor: The Marx Brothers, S. J. Perelman, and Nathanael West." *Southern Review* 12 (July 1976): 659–72. Mostly speculates on the rather uncertain literary relationships between Perelman and West.

Wells, Walter. "Shriek of the Locusts." In *Tycoons and Locusts*. Carbondale: Southern Illinois University Press, 1973, pp. 49–70. In the context of some 1930s Hollywood fictions, this examines West's last novel and perceptively notes important details and their resonances.

Widmer, Kingsley. "The Hollywood Image: Novels About Southern California." *Coastlines Literary Magazine* 5 (1971): 17–27.

————. "The Sweet, Savage Prophecies of Nathanael West." In *The Thirties*, edited by Warren French, pp. 97–106. Deland, Fla.: Everett/Edwards, 1967.

————. "The Last Masquerade: *The Day of the Locust*." In *Nathanael West: The Cheaters and the Cheated*, edited by David Madden, pp. 58–74. Deland, Fla.: Everett/Edwards, 1973.

————. "The Way Down to Wisdom: The Atheism of Celine, Wright and West." In *Edges of Extremity: Some Problems of*

Literary Modernism. University of Tulsa Monographs in Modern
Literature, no. 17. Tulsa, Okla.: University of Tulsa, 1980, pp.
58–74.

Wilson, Edmund. "The Boys in the Back Room." In *A Literary
Chronicle, 1920–1950.* New York: Random House, 1956, pp.
245–49. An influential early (1941) brief discussion of West's
seriousness.

Wyrick, Deborah. "Dadaist Collage Structure and Nathanael West's
Dream Life of Balso Snell." Studies in the Novel 11 (Fall 1979):
349–59. Presents some parallels of the first novel and some
dadaist works.

Zlotnick, Joan. "The Medium Is the Message, Or Is It? A Study of
Nathanael West's Comic Strip Novel." *Journal of Popular Culture* 5 (Summer 1971): 236–40. Pertinent but brief note on
Miss Lonelyhearts relation to satiric artists and West's ironic
"comic strip" analogy since he attacked popular culture.

5. Cassette lecture

Widmer, Kingsley, *The Day of the Locust (Nathanael West).* Twen-
tiethy Century American Novel Cassette Curriculum. Deland, Fla.:
Everett/Edwards, 1970.

Index

DATE DUE		